ANIMAL WATCHING AT NIGHT

There's always an element of excitement when a child is allowed to stay up past their bedtime or is actively encouraged to get up earlier than usual in the morning (this doesn't, however, always work with teenagers as they are often up beyond their curfew and then never surface before noon the following day!). Whilst all wild animal watching is fascinating, being out and about as dawn breaks or dusk falls in search of them is even more so. Nocturnal possibilities include some deer species who feed at dawn and dusk rather than during daytime; badgers, foxes' hedgehogs and of course, owls. Don't forget bats too; observing them in flight and learning more about them as a result, is often enough to prevent an irrational fear of bats which so many people seem to have.

Local naturalists might point you in the right direction of where to go and watch but sometimes it is just a question of being in the right place at the right time – and it's not always necessary to be in the great outdoors as some wildlife are regular garden visitors, or hunt through the local park as it becomes less disturbed by human activity. Badgers in particular are sticklers for routine and will continue using certain paths for generations even though fences and gardens might nowadays replace what were fields in their ancestor's day.

In order to ensure the best chances of success, a little reconnaissance on granddad's part prior to the intended outing might be in order. Tracks regularly used by animals will be quite obvious and sometimes, where they pass under or through a barbed wire fence, it may be possible to see strands of hair left behind. Owls, particularly barn owls are, depending on food availability, also creatures of habit and it one has been seen in a certain area, there's a good chance it will be seen again on another occasion.

Remember to stay downwind of where an animal is most likely to pass by in order that it doesn't catch your scent. Dark clothing obviously helps in remaining undetected but quietness and patience is likely to be rewarded – for this reason, it is not perhaps the best activity for very young children who are likely to become quickly bored. It is always possible to add further to the interest by trying to capture nocturnal wildlife on camera – a totally different challenge to taking images in the daylight.

Always be aware of the extra need for safety at dawn or dusk; that ditch so obvious during daylight hours can be positively dangerous in the dark. Also, beware of the possibility of trespass and any laws regarding the legal rights of animals. It is, for instance, illegal to disturb a badger earth.

CHICKENS AND CHILDREN

At both ends of the age spectrum, keeping chickens is undoubtedly good for you! As far as granddad is concerned, 'HenPower', is a group created by a north of England-based organization who are advocates of creative ageing and providing opportunities for self-expression in order to promote personal well-being. With the birth of HenPower, it was found that by keeping chickens (or at least having some involvement with them) the health of many of the older generation improved; depression and loneliness was reduced – and even the need for some types of medication was lessened.

Children also love chickens – and with good reason. It might be their beautiful feathers and iridescence; their character and company. Far more likely, though, is the way they encourage nurturing: just as soon as you give them your time and attention, they immediately give something back.

Possibly the best thing about chickens is that they can, more or less, fit in to whatever space and location is available. In addition, there is almost certainly a breed or type that will prove suitable. Chickens cannot, however, be kept in cramped and over-crowded conditions and it is important that they are correctly housed and fed. With that in mind, they are the perfect way of teaching children the responsibilities of looking after a pet or livestock… as well as being great fun. And of course, you get eggs for breakfast!

Considering the possibility of chickens; preparing their house and run; finding out about their food requirements and then choosing the birds themselves; can be a great joint venture between grandchildren and granddad.

Perhaps the first thing to decide upon is where the birds are to be kept. If at the child's house then obviously parents will need to become involved and if at granddad's, will the children visit often enough to make the project sufficiently interesting and educational?

Once that decision has been made, suitable housing must be priority. This will undoubtedly be your biggest expense – unless that is, you are fortunate enough to have an existing building or garden shed that can be adapted. Generally though, a specifically designed

THE DANGEROUS BOOK FOR GRANDDADS

INTRODUCTION

There is much in the current media about how children nowadays prefer to play computer games rather than participate in the kind of activities so enjoyed by their parents and grand-parents.

Without the encouragement to climb trees, kick through autumn leaves, collect bugs and paddle about in ditches and streams, the psychologists worry that future generations will succumb to 'epidemic obesity, attention-deficit disorder, isolation and childhood depression.'

Parents busy with work often rely on active retired grandparents to help with child care at the end of the school day, weekends and during school holidays.

Not only are people living longer, they are thinking 'younger' and the modern attitude of mind is that all things are possible. I'm sure that, more than halfway through my sixth decade, I don't think or act like grandparents would have done two or three generations ago… today's maxim must surely be 'You're never too old'!

There is, for some, also the fact that, because of the availability of private pension plans and financial forward thinking by the 'baby-boomers', more 'disposable income' available. Yes, you could leave it to your children and grandchildren as an inheritance, but why miss out on the fun of sharing it in mutual enjoyment? Not that there is need to have money – it is far more important to give quality time.

Grandparents tend to have more time, take a far more relaxed 'been there, done that' attitude and are more lenient than a child's parents. They are also far more likely to indulge their grandchildren with 'forbidden treats' which, once in a while, do no harm at all. As a photo posted on Facebook by AARP Illinois – an organization which is 'leading a revolution in the way people view and live life after 50' – recently stated; 'Grandpas are there to help children get into the mischief that they haven't thought of yet.'!

As a grandparent it would be a shame to miss out on such privileges by not making the most of your grandchildren whilst you can. The very young can be easily entertained by something as simple as a trip to the aquarium section of your local garden centre to see the tanks of fish; a trip down a seaside pier armed with small change to play the old-fashioned slot-machine games or an introduction to an age-appropriate board game battled out on the kitchen table. Sadly, it appears that many rarely get the opportunity to play such games as, with the coming of computer-based entertainment, parents of todays' children have themselves never played a board game. Perhaps now is the time for grandparents to reinstate a fun tradition missed almost entirely by a generation?

Slightly older children can be taught to 'French Skip' or play 'Conkers' – both activities common enough in the school playgrounds of their granddad and grandma. Apparently, the same age group find writing on a chalk-board something of a novelty as, in today's classrooms, computer links to a screen are far more common.

Even notoriously surly young teenagers who might throw up their hands in horror and stomp back to their bedrooms in disgust should a trip out together be suggested by their parents, will happily indulge in an expedition or shed/garage-based project pioneered and put into practice by granddad. Building something with potentially dangerous 'grown-up' tools; camping, exploring and raft-building are all opportunities for hours of interest, excitement and subtle education that would most probably not be otherwise entertained.

Becoming a granddad doesn't, however, mean that you will gain all the skills necessary to enjoy adventures with your grandchildren overnight! For most, it's a case of identifying the basic skills and subsequently learning together. In fact, often being more radical of thought, a youngster may well come up with solutions well before the supposedly more practical and worldly-wise adult! The main thing is 'just do it'.

CHAPTER 1: BIRDS, BEASTS AND BUGS!

'Nobody loves me, everybody hates me
Think I'll go and eat worms
Long ones, short ones, fat ones, thin ones
See how they wriggle and squirm.'

Whether it's because of the slime factor associated with worms; a fear of potentially dangerous foreign, furry spiders, or the cuddly appeal of pets, almost all young children have a fascination with birds, beasts and bugs. As they get older, whilst the reasons for their interest might alter, provided that they've been given encouragement by parents and grandparents along the way, it's unlikely that they will ever lose that initial love and fascination. Whether they will ever want to eat worms is another matter entirely!

house and run is your best option. If you are of a D.I.Y nature, you could perhaps take a sneaky look at the design of one for sale at your nearest suppliers and then build your own.

Other costs include feeders and drinkers. Eventually as you become even more enthusiastic and knowledgeable, you might feel the need to shell out (forgive the pun) on a little incubator and brooder in order to breed from your own stock. Day-to-day essentials are, however, minimal and include not much more than fresh water, a balanced feed suitable for the types of chickens you keep, wood shavings or similar for the floor covering of the house and a few minutes spent morning and evening.

'Forewarned is forearmed', or so goes the old saying. To this end, before buying your first birds, it may pay to join a local poultry/smallholding club. Reading one of the many books available and taking out a regular subscription to one of the chicken-related magazines is also a good idea.

When all is ready and a *reputable* breeder/supplier sourced, make sure that everyone concerned goes and chooses the chickens together. A good and understanding breeder will always encourage potential customers to choose their own birds. As one remarked: 'It's important that anyone – particularly children – who buys birds from me takes home exactly what they want… you choose other pets carefully and for their characteristics so why not your chickens?'

FLYING FALCONS AT THE FAIRS

Helen Macdonald's book, *H is For Hawk* amply demonstrates the fascination many people have for hawks and falcons. Sadly, not many of us have the time, facilities or the knowledge to train our own – but it is possible to experience something of the excitement in the main ring of a country fair or agricultural show where falconry displays are always popular. At most such venues, some children will be invited into the ring to 'help' the falconer… and will find they need nerves of steel as a bird flies fast and low past their face or even onto their gloved hand. The look of pure joy as the children leave the ring to join the adults afterwards, make this an excursion well worth considering.

Because many rural show and city park activities organisers include such a display in their main ring events, it should be possible for the majority of grandparents to take their grandchildren along in order to get up-close and personal. If that's not possible, there's likely to

be a hawk or falconry centre somewhere close to home; many of which organise falconry
'experiences' with children very much in mind.

HORSES FOR COURSES!

Ever fancied being a modern-day John Wayne and trotting off into the sunset sat astride your
mount?! It is undoubtedly more difficult swinging your leg across the saddle after one has
reached the age of 50 plus and, whilst it is unlikely that 'Gramps' will ever be able to tackle the
Grand National course, if it's something that he has never before considered or thought possible,
it's never too late to have a go.

Horse riding has always been popular with children – especially with young girls. For
some, their interest comes as a result of encouragement from their parents or because of being
influenced by the activities of their like-minded peers. Others go off every Saturday morning to
the riding school simply because of a love of ponies and horses that none of their family or
friends share. If that's the case, then perhaps it's time that they encourage their Granddad to take
riding lessons in order that, with competence, both young and old generations can hack out
together – or even enjoy a weekend trekking and camping holiday as is common amongst
grandparents and their grandchildren in the US – sometime in the near future.

KEEPING REPTILES AND SPIDERS

Keeping such things can be as dangerous as you want – although a boa constrictor or a spider
whose venom is known to be deadly is probably a step too far! You will likely require some
specialist equipment and a certain amount of knowledge so it's a pastime that ought to be
considered carefully. However, once it's been decided to take the plunge, it is an enthralling
hobby – and one which teaches children responsibility for something other than themselves. It
also educates; not only as to the geographical locations where the various reptiles and spiders are
found in their natural environment, but also with regards to conservation.

Whenever the word 'conservation' is used, it is natural to think of lions, tigers, elephants
and rhino's but many species of reptiles and spiders are just as vulnerable; so much so that a
growing body of enthusiasts are nowadays actively involved in the reputable breeding and
rearing of home-bred examples in order to bring down the numbers of wild caught ones currently

being captured to supply the ever-popular pet trade. In time, and with experience, you could also help with similar conservation projects.

Basic requirements

The basic requirements are a tank, a heat mat and/or a heat lamp. Spiders don't need a light but some species of lizards will benefit from an ultra-violet light. Although not for the squeamish (but what child of a certain age is squeamish?!), feeding couldn't be easier: spiders might be fed once a week or fortnight depending on the species and snakes and lizards vary immensely (but could be as often as daily or as infrequently as once every three weeks). Spiders are fed on crickets and mealworms, reptiles on frozen (but defrosted) chicks and mice or young rats, and lizards on meat and/or crickets – all of which are readily available from pet shops and are stocked with that particular purpose in mind.

As to time required in their general care and attention, ten minutes a day is all that's needed but the tanks might need cleaning every couple of months. It's possible to buy bacteria-free soil for the base of the tanks whilst the vegetation included to make the environment as natural as possible can consist of either live and/or artificial plants – the latter being required for lizard species that eat live locust which, when released into a tank of growing plants, will strip the leaves overnight!

Beginners to snake-keeping should start with either a corn snake or a royal python (which should be obtained at a young age so that they become accustomed to handling) whilst the best types of spiders to begin with are three from the tarantula family: the Chilean rose; the Mexican red knee and the Brazilian black. A bearded dragon will satisfy the needs of the would-be lizard keeper!

VOLUNTEER ON A CITY FARM

It's a rare child that doesn't like animals, and farm livestock in particular seem to pique their interest. Maybe it's all those childhood stories from authors such as Dick King-Smith or the old tales of 'Chicken-Licken' but whatever the reason, most get excited at the prospect of a farm visit – hence the success of children's farms and petting zoos.

Somewhat bizarrely, apart from 'Open Farm Sunday' (usually held in June in the UK) and the odd 'Open Day' organized by commercial farmers or agricultural colleges, it is probably easier to get up close and personal with the animals on a city farm than it is those that live in a traditional rural environment out in the countryside. There are undoubtedly practical reasons for this being the case – safety and the risk of transferring disease, being just two – but the fact remains that city farms are definitely easier to contact and access.

So popular are they that some city farms actually have a waiting list of would-be volunteers; others however, have not and will welcome any help that a granddad and his grandchild/children can offer on a regular basis. And what a perfect opportunity to indulge in a love of animals, to discover where our food comes from, learn various life skills, bash and bang with hammer and nails, or simply to get muddy and dirty without anyone telling you off!

It's not just a British thing either. City farms are equally as popular in the US where they too encourage volunteers and offer tuition in animal husbandry and vegetable growing. Often run on a non-profit making basis, some even supply the high-end restaurants and shops and by doing so, are the perfect place for adult and child alike to learn all about getting produce from the garden to the dinner plate – from one fork to another, as it were!

CHAPTER 2: BISH, BASH, BOSH – BUILD SOMETHING!

If you look online for a definition of 'bish, bash, bosh', you're likely to find several explanations as to its origin and meaning. Most, however, think it best ascribed to demonstrate the ease and efficiency with which something has been created. Perfect then to use as this particular section heading as, with a little planning, forethought and enthusiasm, it should be easily possible for any of the following to be completed by 'Team Granddad' and his willing helpers!

BUILD A BIRD BOX AND INSECT HOTEL

Research seems to show that the controlling factor for bird populations (and some insects) is not food, but the availability of nesting sites. In the interest of conservation as well as being a fun, fascinating and educational thing to do together, building, erecting and maintaining a few bird boxes and/or insect hotels could be a good joint project. Not only does the bird and insect population benefit; there's the added pleasure of being able to observe the comings and goings from a safe distance, or even, if of a technical mind, via a camcorder which can be watched indoors on a lap-top.

Bird boxes

Depending on what birds' one wishes to attract, it should be possible to download specific plans from the internet.

You can make a nesting box out of many materials but, arguably, you cannot better plywood. Modern plywood uses a glue for the laminates which is resistant to weather and, if treated properly it will last for many years. It's simple to work and can be coated to help reduce its visual impact in the wild. Use plywood that is about 1cm thick (approximately ½ in)… they can be made from thinner ply but it makes nailing the pieces together a little more difficult. Your local DIY store will cut it to size for you but first enquire if they sell 'off-cuts' – the smaller pieces of the sheet that remain after they have cut pieces for other customers. If you explain what you want them for, you may find they will give some to you, or at least charge very little.

As to siting a nest box, it is very much a question of trial and error. I once constructed one late in the season and, intending to place it elsewhere, simply hung it on a fence panel to dry only a short distance from the house window. Within 24 hours, a pair of blue tits had taken up residence! Generally, though, most bird boxes should be fixed about head height, under the eaves of a shed or in a tree with the entrance hole away from any prevailing wind.

Who will use it? Most of the tit family, but you may even be lucky enough to have a tree-creeper nest in it. If so, leave well alone as they are very shy and may abandon the nest if disturbed – so watch from a distance.

The Best Exotic Insect Hotel!

Even the smallest garden hosts a multitude of fascinating bugs and insects – but there could be even more if they are given a helping hand. An insect hotel can be as large or as small as you like: some might be rather grand made out of pallets, logs, old house bricks and all manner of things, but a just small open-ended box filled with lengths of straw – both natural and the waxed drinking type – will be a desirable residence for some. Try and tilt the front slightly so that any water can drain out.

Holes drilled in a block of wood – which is then attached to a fence or wall in a sheltered part of the garden – will often be used by various types of flying insects that enter in order to lay their eggs and then plug up the entrance hole with dirt or mud until the eggs hatch. A small, neatly stacked pile of straight branch lengths or thin logs is all that's required for many insects –

and as the wood slowly rots and decays, it will become suitable for even more. A pile of logs might even become home to hedgehogs' who will use it for winter hibernation, and even if they don't, they'll certainly feed on some of the grubs and insects to be found there.

BOAT BUILDING IN THE GARAGE

Everyone knows the tale of the man who built a sailing dinghy in his cellar and then couldn't get it out through the door! Before considering constructing a boat in the garage, you do, in all seriousness, need to make sure that it will fit – and that once completed, it can be taken out through the entrance. For this reason, the majority of granddads will only ever be able to contemplate a rowing boat or possibly a Mirror dinghy – but for ideas and beautiful models (of the marine variety!) one could do worse than take a look the internet and boat-building magazines – of which there are a plethora. Once complete, a boat can give both Granddad and grandchildren hours of fun – and that element of measured danger. Read *Swallows and Amazons* to your grandchildren so as to stimulate enthusiasm and, if there isn't a safe body of water nearby on which to safely sail your boat, then scale things down a little.

Bearing in mind all the possible potential problems involved in building a full-scale boat, it might be more practical for 'Team Granddad' to consider a model boat, built either from scratch or as a restoration project. Pond yachts, in various state of disrepair sometimes turn up at car-boot sales; auctions and could even be discovered neglected in a relative's shed or garage.

Granddad and even Granddad's dad may well have had a pond yacht in their youth. They were very popular in the 1920s, '30s and '40s and were designed to be used in urban parks; most of which incorporated a shallow boating pond. The fact that they were quite shallow was probably a good thing as some of these boats were not all that well balanced and would tip over in a strong gust of breeze – necessitating the removal of shoes and socks and the rolling up of trousers in order to go and retrieve them! Some, however, were finely crafted works of art and, at the height of their popularity, many conformed to class ratings and were raced in competitions.

There is definitely something very attractive and enticing about sailing a pond yacht; as American, Wiley Reynolds, maker of Challenger model yachts is quoted as saying: '…if you seek relaxation, just going for a sail is marvellously peaceful. Once the boats in the water out on a journey, you are in its world. It is a real sailboat, just a small one. It is also a wonderful activity to do with your friends, children or grandchildren, and then of course it is not really about the boat, but the companionship.'

If even pond yachts are not a practical option, then it's possible to scale things down even further by building a whole fleet of Spanish Armada type miniature sailing boats from the shells of walnuts!

Carefully crack open the nuts so that you are left with two halves and then remove the kernels. At the base of each half, in the centre, fix a blob of plasticine or Blu-Tack. Make paper sails in the shape of those used at the time of the Armada and gently push a cocktail stick or toothpick through at top and bottom so as to create the look of a billowing sail. Press one end of the stick into the plasticine and you're ready to do battle in paddling pool or bathtub!

BUILD A SHED

A garden shed can become a place of many adventures and is the perfect place to carry out hobbies and activities. It's been said that a shed is like a lady's handbag – both contain all the essentials for survival in the modern world and both are private and personal sanctuaries!

Everybody needs a shed – and it's almost compulsory if you are a granddad. Back in the mists of time, he could always be found around his shed on the allotment, or in the one at the bottom of the garden where he tinkered, cleaned his gardening tools – and hid from 'grandma'! To any child, such a place had an immediate attraction and was explored and investigated at any and every opportunity.

A shed is equally as important today; it's a place in which to work and construct things without worrying about making a mess and, with modern grandparents being generally far fitter and more active than their predecessors', the perfect storage for bicycles, scuba-diving equipment or whatever other paraphernalia might be required to pursue a hobby or pastime. As far as grandchildren are concerned, it's a great place for making some of the many things described within these pages and also for carrying out 'dangerous' and dirty experiments – of which more later!

Traditionally, most sheds were made of wood and protected from the elements by roofing felt. Windows were, in many cases, adapted from a previous life and there was always a distinct smell of creosote! Today, an 'off-the-peg' model will be the favoured option for most – either supplied in sections for the DIY enthusiast, or delivered and erected by the suppliers – but, as a combined granddad/grandchild project, why not make a shed yourself?

There are a few points to bear in mind, firstly, location and area. Your shed should be on flat ground; but obviously not at the bottom of a slope for fear of flooding. Where possible, it also ought to be south-facing. As to the area, make sure that the space available is adequate for the inclusion of a shed that is going to be 'fit for purpose' bearing in mind the fact that the outside dimensions will need to include roof overhang, the probable provision of a water-butt/drainage to take away rainwater.

Next is the subject of light and/or electricity – natural lighting can often be gained by the inclusion of sky-lights in the roof as well as conventional side windows but, for all those things planned, a source of electricity is likely to be essential. It needs to be 'fit for purpose' too – a bank of plugs may be sufficient for some things but a more substantial source will be required if it is intended to work a heavy-duty lathe or similar equipment.

Finally, some form of heating might be required for the colder months. A solar panel on the roof could help solve all these problems – as will good insulation. Roof insulation will help in keeping the temperature ambient.

No shed needs to be boring to look at! Assuming that one doesn't contravene and local housing restrictions and regulations, let your imagination run wild! In the 'Shed of the Year' competition held annually in the UK, examples of entries include a backwoodsman's cabin; environmentally-friendly sheds built totally from recycled materials' Dr. Who's 'Tardis'; an old rural garage; clubhouse, bars and a beach hut. If there's not a similar competition where you are, then you could always start one or, at the very least set up a blog about how you went about building your shed and any subsequent shed-based activities!

No shed needs to be boring when it comes to its more obscure usage either! As well as some of the more conventional shed-based activities, or using it as a base for a model railway, why not play the part of the 'Mad Professor' and introduce your grandchild to the world of science and 'dangerous' experiments that create small explosions and other dramatic effects?

Whilst it's easy to picture a cartoon image of bubbling apparatus, multi-coloured smoke emerging from under the door and windows and, in true Tom and Jerry style, the shed itself blasting into smithereens, such experiments need only be 'dangerous' in the child's eyes!

Online, or in book form, you can, believe it or not, find out exactly how to make slime; create glow-in-the-dark gherkins; make a rocket, or even a teabag, fly; build a static electricity flea circus; erect a homemade power station; construct a can crusher; create a hologram; make square bubbles or extract DNA from food!

Continuing the 'mad scientist' theme, a section of the work bench could become a temporary biology lab where mini-beasts and insects from the garden are looked at through a magnifying glass or a cheap microscope/lens (before then being returned to their natural environment).

Sheds as dens

And then there are sheds built for no other purpose than as children's dens. Space, practicality and finance might cause restrictions, but there are no such confines on a child's imagination and it is crucial that they play an important part in the ideas and design. Granddad can plant the seed but then let the grandchildren run with it: drawn plans and internet research are all helpful to the project.

The British gardening writer and broadcaster, Bunny Guinness suggests using old hazel, willow and trellis panels as the basis for a den and says that she once saw an old dog kennel that had been converted into a tree house. She also makes the point that privacy is important to a child. With that in mind, an old dinghy 'blocked up' safely in the corner of the garden forms an ideal base on which to build a cabin section from where pirate games can begin or, if in quiet completive mood, a safe haven in which to read a book.

A fort or army garrison takes little more than a few wooden delivery palettes stood on end and secured with posts strategically driven into the ground whilst if a suitable tree exists, a palette or two can be hoisted up into its branches as a platform for a tree house.

It wouldn't be unreasonable to assume that you need a tree in order to be able to construct a tree-house… but you'd be wrong! Obviously if there is one in the garden that is strong enough and has large, spreading branches, things are definitely that much easier but even without anything at all arboreal in sight, it's possible to build a 'tree' house on stilts something similar to a watch tower. The main thing is that it should be a private place and, by pulling up a rope ladder, will repel invaders, or, that it fires a child's imagination and encourages games with their friends.

Give a child a saw, hammer and nails and a pile of timber and they will most likely be too impatient to consider plans and design as it's a natural reaction to want to get going and see what develops! A plan is, however, quite a good idea – you could even build a scale model out of cardboard just to see how things might look.

Tree houses can be constructed from reclaimed wood – but be sure to have removed all the old nails or things that could harm – or made from timber bought especially for the purpose. A solid base and frame must be the main thing and from this beginning, almost any design is possible. One should, though, bear a few points in mind:

* Never nail or screw directly into a tree – always build a frame around its trunk or a platform over its branches. As well as not damaging the tree, doing so also keeps the swaying on a windy day from pulling apart the structure.

* Be aware of any possible preservation orders on mature trees.

* Consider what the tree house will look like if viewed from the roadside or from a neighbours' window or garden.

* As with many things, size is important – both from the point of what the tree branches can stand weight-wise, and also with regard to the confines of your garden.

GO-CART BUILDING

In the area of England where I grew up, go-carts made from pram wheels and wood, steered by a bolt-pivoted cross-piece and a loose rein of light rope was known as either a 'hurry-cart' or 'lorry-cart'. Elsewhere they might be known as 'bogies' More universal, though, is the term 'go-cart'.

As simple or as sophisticated as you like, without doubt, the best go-karts are homemade from a few old planks, wooden offcuts and a couple of pairs of wheels. Pram wheels of the right kind are nowadays difficult to get hold of unless someone happens to still have a 'Silver Cross' type tucked away somewhere (in which case I doubt they'll be too happy if you were to demolish it for the sake of the wheels!) but suitable alternatives might be found in the shape of discarded bicycle, or even golf-buggy wheels.

In my day (and how often do even the youngest thinking granddads use that expression as they approach pension age!), it was enough to sit on the flat boards; nonetheless, even the most basic of designs can be improved by an appropriate amount of comfort. A reasonable seat can be created by removing the legs of an old chair, but make sure it is firmly fixed to the main chassis in order to avoid the possibility of the driver going one way and the go-cart another when turning on a particularly sharp corner.

Possibly the best thing about building a go-kart is the opportunity it gives 'Gramps' and his grandchildren to spend time together. Perhaps it might be possible to build two – a 'little and large', if you like – and to create a competitive element in both their construction and their subsequent use on the 'racetrack'.

CHAPTER 3: COMPETITION CHALLENGE

Some kind granddads deliberately 'throw' a game of cards or board game so as to encourage the youngsters with whom they are playing. Take the same competitive element one stage further however, and the situation seems to change. Whilst he might be outwardly encouraging, it would appear there's a definite need to win on granddad's part!

AN 'IMPOSSIBLE TASKS' CHALLENGE

Set your grandchildren a seemingly 'impossible' challenge (perhaps with some clues) to complete within a day/week/summer holiday and then your grandchildren can set an 'impossible' task for Granddad. Perhaps there can even be a trophy offered for the winner and it be competed for on a regular basis throughout the year. For example, one such challenge could be to find naturally sourced materials for pen, paper and ink. Include a clue such as 'Who needs to text-message when it's possible to find all you need to write a letter out in the woods?' and then let your grandchild's imagination work out any possible permutations.

Giving the listener a very unfair advantage, the answer to the above is, on a walk, seek out a primary (one of the first ten on a bird's wing) or tail feather from a pigeon or rook – you don't need to be in the countryside to do this as they can frequently be found in the garden or local park. Then, with a penknife, carefully slice the end off, cut the tip square and slit it until it resembles the nib of a fountain pen.

Find a silver birch tree (preferably not in your local park or municipal garden!) and, with the penknife, carefully score a square and peel of the bark; taking care not to strip the bark from all round the trunk of the tree. The inner side of the bark is quite smooth and forms your 'paper'.

Making sure that you have correctly identified them (a good book is *Mushroom and Other Fungi* by Eleanor Lawrence and Sue Hariness), find either the common inkcap or shaggy inkcap toadstool, inside either of which can be found a black inky fluid…

GROW THE BIGGEST PUMPKIN AND SUNFLOWER

Traditionally, Granddads' have allotments, and allotments grow pumpkins (and much else besides). However, even without such space, a small part of most gardens can be allocated to growing the biggest or the tallest.

Growing a pumpkin in a very small area might not be all that practical as their tendrils tend to spread out somewhat. They can, however, be 'trained' to go more or less where you want them and if you are only intending growing one or two plants it ought to be possible to find sufficient space somewhere. Buy your small plants from the garden centre or, ideally, grow them from seed – they need to be set at least 1metre (3ft) apart when planted out. To help achieve the biggest pumpkin, nip out the tips of the shoots once they are about 45cm (18in) long and if the fruit isn't forming, try assisting pollination by transferring pollen from male to female flowers with a small artist's paintbrush (the female flowers are the ones with slightly swollen bases). To stand the best chance of growing the biggest, use varieties such as 'Hundredweight' and 'Big Max'.

All children (and many bees and butterflies) love sunflowers. Grow them from seeds in pots on the kitchen windowsill and then, when all danger of frost has passed, plant them out about 60cm (2ft) apart in a sheltered but sunny part of the garden (alternatively, you may prefer to keep them in a large pot rather than directly in the soil). To grow the tallest, you need to choose varieties such as 'Mammoth' or 'Giant Yellow' and make sure they are tied to a stake as they mature in order that a strong wind or even heavy rain cannot damage them.

Many local flower and vegetable shows have classes for children as well as adults so find out the date of this year's show, contact the secretary and ask to be sent a schedule so you can see for which classes your pumpkins and sunflowers may be eligible. Make sure you have followed the relevant guidelines in the schedule before putting your pumpkin in the wheelbarrow and trundling off down the road accompanied by gasps of amazement from your neighbours!

If there isn't a local show, then why not arrange your own with other granddads' and grandchildren in the area? And there's no need to confine yourselves to pumpkins and sunflowers either. There are many interesting and unusual-looking vegetables so it ought to be possible to organise classes showcasing the biggest, the heaviest, the tallest and the ugliest. If you can get a local gardening expert involved so much the better; not only could he offer advice during the growing season, he would be the perfect impartial judge for your show.

HIT 'BULLS-EYE'

Hitting the bulls'-eye on a target wasn't just a competitive game for those of Medieval times – many ordinary men were required to practice archery by law in readiness for the day when they might be needed to go into battle and fight for king and country. The first ever such law in England was passed in 1252 and dictated that all Englishmen aged between 15-60 should own a bow and arrows and spend a certain amount of time each week improving their archery skills. There's no reason at all why Granddad and grandchild shouldn't hone *their* skills and embark on a competition in the garden that involves the use of various targets and a variety of 'weapons'!

Making a bow and arrow from a piece of whippy hazel or willow cut fresh from the wood, a length of suitable string slightly shorter than the length of bow, and a few arrows fashioned from hazel stems and topped out with a flight made of card or feathers, is something most granddads will have done in their childhood.

If you can't get out into the countryside, depending on what's growing in the garden or on ground near to home, it might still be possible to find suitable materials with which to make a bow – even if, on its own, a length of growth is too thin and not robust enough. In such a situation, you could try making what is sometimes referred to as a 'bundle bow' from three or more thin wands of unequal length and thickness that are held together by strong tape or tightly whipped with thin string. The longest wands should be in the centre of the bundle and the shorter ones around its centre to create a thicker 'belly' at the point where the archer will hold it prior to firing.

Fresh, green wood will make a bow that can be used straightaway but it is unlikely to be as efficient as a seasoned one and it may stay bent once unstrung. A little bit of drying time will make the chosen wood stronger and most types are dry enough to turn into a bow within two or three weeks of natural drying.

The simplest of bows requires the whippy stem cut twice as long as the user's 'draw length' (the greatest distance between the back of the bow and the bow string when the bow is fully drawn) which usually equates to a bow length nearly as tall as the user. For very small children a bow length shorter than this might be more suitable as they have less power needed and are easier to use.

Carve notches towards each end of the bow as these will help the string remain in place during use. You could even cut a stick for the bow which has a small fork at one end, in which case, looping the string so that it rests in the fork will save the need to cut one of the notches. Tightly tie the string at one end and then pull it until the bow forms a crescent shape. To work out just how far to bend it, it may be useful to know that some people use a gap of one 'fistmele' (a word that has lasted since the Medieval archers) – a fistmele being the distance between the top of your thumb and the bottom of your fist when you give a thumbs-up sign. Tie the loose end around the other notch. One advantage of using a stick that is forked at one end is that, once the length of string has been determined, you can make a loop in the string and 'hook' the loop over the fork – making it easier to undo when the bow is not in use.

Arrows can be made from thin dowelling but, in the spirit of adventure, it is far more satisfying to make one's own from natural shoots taken from wherever you got your bow length. Point one end and at the other, cut a 'nock' that is just the right width to lightly grip the bow string. Smooth the nock so that it doesn't fray the string when in use.

Most arrows have flights made from feathers (either chicken, pigeon, crow or similar). Three flights are normally used but some use only two (but then, just to be awkward, others fit their arrows with four!). Cut a section of feather about 8cm (3in) long and tear some of the long barbs off each end of the quill, leaving a central section of about 4cm (1½in) still entire. Split the feather in half along the quill to make two sections. Place one section on each side of the nock end of your arrow and fix it with tape or by whipping cotton thread around them. Alternatively, make flights from thick cardboard or even lengths of adhesive cut, fashioned and attached as one would the more traditional feather variety.

A quick glance at *Wikipedia* will tell you that a 'trebuchet is a type of catapult that was used as a siege engine in the Middle Ages. Making model trebuchets is very popular in schools in both the UK and US, indeed, there are competitions held which are fiercely contested between different schools and colleges. Competition rules vary but may include the fact that the trebuchet can be built by a team of two or three pupils and must have an arm designed to throw a softball as far as possible. Height and 'launch box' size are also stipulated within the rules; as is the fact that the device must be able to be cocked by one person. Also, no explosions or air pressure may be used and the power used to project the ball must be provided by the machine itself.

As such, a trebuchet could be an appropriate inclusion in several sections of this book as it would, for instance, be a good thing to build in the garden shed – as well as fitting quite well here when discussing the competitive element! For now, though, the catapults to which we refer are the ones sometimes known as sling-shots, favoured by both David when he killed Goliath and the 'Outlaws', who were the hero's friends in the *Just William* books written by Richmal Crompton.

Penknives and catapults were in almost every boy's pocket during granddad's childhood and it's likely that he will need no encouragement or instructions to make a simple catapult from a forked stick cut from the hedgerow. However, just to refresh a possibly aging memory, a few reminders might be in order!

* Seek out and cut (with a small saw for preference) a forked stick already growing in the rough shape of a traditional catapult – carve or otherwise shape it if the forks or 'handle' are not exactly as they should be – remove the bark and, if impatient grandchildren will allow, leave it to season for a month or two.

* Sand the catapult down for comfort and then attach fairly strong square or flat elastic (available online via Amazon, eBay or catapult suppliers… or, cut your own from an old tyre inner tube). Tying the elastic directly to the prongs is the easiest way but doing so makes the trajectory unpredictable and it is best to first bind a strong, short piece of leather to each prong and then attach the elastic to these.

* Before fixing the elastic, you may like to take another piece of softer leather (the tongue of an old shoe!); cut two slits and thread it onto the elastic so as to create a pouch or holding pocket into which the intended missile can be held between finger and thumb before being released.

Hitting the Target – Safety First

Any budding Robin Hood and his Merry Men can make targets from cardboard in the shape of rabbits, deer, wild boar or even wolves, whilst the William Tell fan might like to balance an apple, tin-can or similar on the top of a gate post! Others may be keen to introduce the competitive element and use a traditional target shape with different coloured rings and a bulls'-eye. Points can be awarded for accuracy – the nearer the bull, the higher the score.

You can do the same for catapult-aiming targets. Another idea would be to collect the plastic 'squeezable' bottles that have previously held tomato ketchup, salad dressing and the like. All lined up in a row in the manner of a coconut shy, they make excellent targets as their wide, flat front and backs provide a good point at which to aim. For further fun, as they are almost human shape with their cap 'heads', short necks and 'body'-like bottles, they could be painted and decorated to look like pirates or enemy troops!

With all of the above, safety is, of course, paramount. Targets should never be placed in such a way that an errant arrow or catapult missile could ever go so wide of the mark that it is a danger to neighbours', animals or property. To be doubly safe, erect a curtain of hessian or garden windbreak behind the targets which will 'kill' the speed of anything fired. Finally, if you are entertaining more than one child, always ensure that each has laid down their bows before any go to collect their arrows.

OVERCOMING OBSTACLES'

As children, many of us fixed a rope from a tree and swung on it over a stream or muddy ditch. Likewise, an obstacle course of varying degrees of difficulty might have been designed by our young, fearless minds. The consequences were almost inevitable!

Whilst some such challenges are is impossible to achieve in the average suburban back garden (unless Granddad really has been neglecting his garden maintenance and cultivation of late!), you could, nonetheless, create your own mini assault course using the obligatory rope and a simplified version of the types of obstacles one might find on the average army training ground. Make them sturdy enough to carry an adult's weight and take it in turn to see who can get round the course in the quickest time!

With no garden at all, if there's a country park near you, it's quite likely that there will be an obstacle course over which you can test your athletic prowess; otherwise, take your grandchildren to the local playground and organize a competitive challenge there by itemizing the sequence of obstacles (climbing frame; zip-wire; slide etcetera) over which competitors have to clamber against the clock. Unfortunately, because of the by-laws appertaining to children's play equipment, it is unlikely that adults will be allowed to participate – a fact for which you may or may not be grateful!

WHEELING AND DEALING

Due to the popularity of television antique 'buying and selling' programmes, everyone thinks they are an expert when it comes to finding a bargain and selling it on for a profit. Granddads' can encourage an interest in history – and introduce an element of risk – by allocating a grandchild a small sum of money and then both going off to a car-boot sale or similar before then taking what was bought to a small provincial auction house in order to see if there's a profit to be made. If there is, use the money to invest in another adventure or to raise money for charity.

There's a most definite competitive element here, as it's one where age and experience doesn't necessarily overcome youthful enthusiasm. Children buy what they like; adults with a view to what might make a profit – quite often children buy 'quirky' whilst adults buy 'quality' and, in the auction room, buyers regularly buy things on a whim; items that make them smile or remind them of their own childhood. Add variation by seeing who can buy or find the most gruesome, tacky or bizarre object for a limited amount of money!

Unless they are very disciplined, every member of each generation collects or inherits personal memorabilia – much of which is designated to the attic or garage, rarely to see the light of day again until such times that they are passed on to the next. A 'Wheeling and Dealing' competitive challenge could be just the perfect opportunity to clear that attic or cupboard under the stairs. Be prepared for disruption and diversion as you do so; children are extremely inquisitive so be ready to answer what might be awkward personal questions – after all, the expression, 'a skeleton in the cupboard' must have come from somewhere!

CHAPTER 4: CURIOUSER AND CURIOUSER!

At the very beginning of chapter two in Lewis Carroll's, *Alice's Adventures in Wonderland,* Alice exclaimed that her experiences were becoming 'curiouser and curiouser'. Bearing in mind what was happening to her, she had every reason to do so – and might well have said the same had she been observing any of the following activities which could be potentially undertaken by almost any grandfather and grandchild in today's modern world!

William Heath Robinson was an early 20th century illustrator who put many of his far-fetched and often totally impractical inventions and ideas into cartoon form. The principle behind many of his inventions was to deliberately make things over-complicated and to solve nonexistent problems such as pancake-making and peeling potatoes! Undoubtedly clever in their design, they were however, makeshift in their construction. Nick Park, the genius behind the highly watchable Wallace & Gromit animations admits to being influenced by Heath Robinson and is on record as saying that all of Wallace's inventions are designed around the principle of using 'a sledgehammer to crack a nut' – a cliché that describes Heath Robinson's work beautifully!

With the aid of string, tape, kebab sticks, rubber bands, cotton reels to use as pulleys and virtually anything one can find around the house, why not try designing and building a working Heath Robinson contraption. If you are feeling more adventurous, do the same – but on a larger scale – either outdoors or in the shed using rope, hammer and nails, curtain tracking, old bicycle wheels, hosepipe and discarded vacuum cleaner parts. The more ridiculous and un-necessary the invention, the better the sense of achievement!

Alongside designing and building a 'Heath Robinson' contraption, you could try creating a museum of nonsense – the more ridiculous the 'exhibits' the better. At Herrnbaumgarten, an hour's drive from Vienna in Austria, there's just such a place. It claims to be the only one of its type in the world but, with imagination and some radical thinking, you might be able to prove them wrong!

In that particular museum, they have a vast collection of silly yet brilliant inventions ranging from a soup plate with a plug so that you can drain the food when you've had enough, right through to a see-through suitcase for nudists. One of the best exhibits, however, must be 'the world's one and only collection of famous button holes', concealed inside (empty) little square boxes with transparent lids!

ROLL A PAINTED EASTER EGG AND CHASE A CHEESE!

At certain times of the year, in some countries, there are some rather peculiar traditions and customs – in just a few of which granddad and his grandchildren might like to get involved. For some reason, Britain seems to have more than its fair share of madcap activities. Take, for instance, the custom of egg-rolling at Easter.

In some places in the north-east of the UK these eggs are known as Pace-eggs. In days gone by, pace-egging would take the form of groups of men wandering around the locality; one of whom would have blackened his face with soot and be carrying a basket; the idea being that he and his happy band of followers would persuade villagers to throw boiled eggs into it. When the pace-eggers had received sufficient quantities, they would stop and perform either a short play or dance. These stops were conveniently planned so as to occur outside the local inn or the home of a person known to be generous in their hospitality! Meeting a rival band could lead to a fair amount of banter, during which one group often attempted to steal the others' basket of eggs.

But if you want real danger, look no further! Be sure to complete a risk assessment before attending any of the several cheese-rolling events generally held in May – careering down a steep hill in pursuit of a Double Gloucester cheese or, as an onlooker, having one coming towards you at full pelt having been released from the top of a hill is definitely bad for your health!

Just three places in Britain where this takes place are Cooper's Hill in Brockworth, Gloucestershire; Stroud, Gloucestershire, and Stilton, near Peterborough, Leicestershire. For egg rolling, try Holcombe Hill, Ramsbottom, Lancashire; the castle moat at Penrith; Bunker's Hill, Derbyshire; Arthur's Seat in Edinburgh and, further afield, the White House lawns, Washington, USA where the annual Easter egg roll is open to children, parents – and their grandparents.

SCARY SCARECROWS

Sometimes it can be great fun to make a scarecrow for the garden and/or as a 'guy' on Bonfire Night. Dangerous? Well, it might be if you decide to make it in the image of an unpopular neighbour or school teacher and your effigy is so lifelike that a person recognizes themselves and doesn't like what they see!

The chance of someone identifying themselves as your model notwithstanding, the ideal scarecrow should be as realistic as a few sticks, some stuffing and a bundle of old clothes can make him (or her) and, if you are making one for its traditional purpose, it should be doing something that is recognizably human – standing upright in the middle of the vegetable patch with both arms outstretched is not a recognized human activity and no doubt the birds will soon be treating it with the contempt it deserves. Instead, add accessories that make it look as if it is holding a stick, waving a flag or even, at its feet, include another scarecrow in the form of a cat or dog. And if your efforts are really too good to stay hidden away in the back garden, why not start a 'Best Scarecrow' completion in your street or village?

There's nowadays many a town and village that organizes an annual scarecrow festival – in which, should you live close enough, you'd be mad not to participate.

Scarecrows first appeared on the streets rather than in the fields, in Kettlewell, Yorkshire, in the early 1990s, since which time several similar festivals have become an annual fixture throughout the country. Often themed, the imagination of local residents seems to know no bounds and so it is that one might bump into ideas spawned by popular 'reality' television programmes of the time. Others include clever plays on words; a group of 'cereal' killers or a platoon of harvest scarecrows led by an army 'kernel'. One, seen some years ago may have been the cleverest, most effective and certainly the simplest – entitled 'Scarecrow on Holiday', the effigy was nothing more than a basic wooden cross. At one time, Thornton Hough, in the Wirrel, Cheshire, held the world record for the most scarecrows in one place, but unfortunately lost the honour to a village in Portugal very shortly afterwards. The appeal of scarecrows is, it seems, worldwide!

LOST YOUR MARBLES?!

Granddads' everywhere must have indulged in their childhood, but don't be fooled into thinking that the sport of marbles which you enjoyed in the school playground is anything like the championship games played at Tinsley Green, West Sussex, each Good Friday – this is a serious contest as befits any form of world championship and as such, has its own rules, rituals and vocabulary. Anywhere else you would be greeted by a bewildered look were you to mention 'nose-drops', 'knuckling down', 'fudging' and 'cabbaging' but at the Greyhound pub, your wise words will be immediately understood. And just in case you might be doubting the authenticity of the 'World Championship' title, it's as well to know that past contestants have come from the US and Algeria – and that Germany has won this particular world war six times.

Although marbles might have been played in the schoolyard for many generations, how many of today's children have a special marble bag containing gloriously coloured tiny glass spheres (and the odd metal ball-bearing with which to cheat and smash the opposition!)? It seems that granddads' worldwide need to bring back the pleasures of marbles and teach that particular winning thumb flick in order to win the battle!

<u>CHAPTER 5: EARTH, WIND AND FIRE</u>

Granddad might know 'Earth, Wind and Fire' as being the name of an American band founded in Chicago in 1969 but to most, it refers to three of the four elements – the fourth being water. There's no denying the fascination of those elemental things. We warn children for messing about with them but what adult can resist the temptation too?!

The best fire is the most primitive, the one that burns outdoors…combine those primeval urges with practicality and, local council legislation permitting, use the activity to tidy up the garden or allotment.

THE ART OF MAKING A BONFIRE

Good bonfires don't just happen, they are carefully constructed with small stuff at the bottom and then, when that is blazing well, with the addition of intermediate-sized offcuts. Any big branches should be put on last, always taking care that the 'bottom' doesn't burn out and, as a result, there is nothing between ground and branch with which to keep the flames flying skywards. If there are big hedge trimmings to deal with then a windless day is best in order that the flames go straight through the pile and are not continually swept to one side. If, on the hand, it is to be half-dried weeds and similar to be burned, a brisk wind is needed so as to blow through the pile and draw oxygen to its centre.

Eager to get going, a grandchild will no doubt suggest starting the conflagration with firelighters, barbeque fuel or even petrol or diesel – DON'T! Not only is it potentially *too* dangerous, it takes away some of the traditional skills required in the art of bonfire making. Instead use scrunched up newspaper (or possibly straw if it's available), and around it, place dry twigs or thin pieces of wood placed upright and leaning teepee-fashion. As the fire takes hold, slowly but surely add more and more wood of ever-increasing size.

Even despite the greatest care and attention, sometimes a fire burns and sometimes it doesn't… but then that's the fun of it!

FORECAST THE WEATHER

Before embarking on a mission, dangerous or not, it's sometimes quite useful to know what the weather is likely to be doing. Yes, of course, in this day and age, you can get a fairly accurate weather forecast from television, radio, the internet or a mobile phone 'app' – but where's the fun in that?!

You could make a weather station (and there are various websites giving suggestions) but it's far more entertaining to use traditional methods such as keeping a piece of seaweed by the back door as a barometer (If the seaweed is moist and/or pliable, the air is probably humid, or a storm is approaching but if it's dry and brittle, the weather is likely to be dry). There are also the old sayings like; 'red sky at night, shepherd's delight; red sky in the morning, shepherd's warning' and, to be a good natural weather forecaster, you really do need to be up as early as possible in the morning for it is the first few hours of the day that are most likely to indicate what's likely to follow.

In summer the early dew soaks the grass, in winter the grass and even the trees are white with frost. If the frost fades quickly, or there is no dew a change is on the way. But if the day continues fine, the horizon not too sharp, the sky soft, and the sun sinks in an even red glow the fine weather will continue.

Watch the activities of the animals, birds and insects. Some can hear thunder long before humans can – a pheasant, for instance will 'cock-up' at the first signs many miles away whilst bees become agitated and desperate to return to the hive. Many insects hatch in warm or humid weather and cattle on the run with their tales up are not frightened by an impending storm but more because of the warble flies which hatch under such conditions. With a storm heading their way, many animals and birds become restless and even Granddad's rheumatic joints might begin to ache!

THUNDER, LIGHTNING – AND ALL THINGS FRIGHTENING!

In the mid-1700s, during a thunderstorm, Benjamin Franklin effectively trapped lightning in a jar when he flew a kite attached to which was attached a key and a silk ribbon. Lucky not to have killed himself, his experiment did, however, answer some questions regarding a force of nature which was once thought by our forebears to have come from the hand of God.

Young and old are all fascinated by thunder and lightning. Go outdoors somewhere safe and watch an amazing free light show – and then try and learn more about the different types of lightning you've witnessed! Alternatively, if it occurs at night, sit indoors in a conservatory or sun room with the lights out and tell each other scary stories – or create the most imaginative explanations for the noise; a giant walking angrily across the clouds, for example!

Tornadoes and hurricanes are more likely to occur in certain areas of the world than others. In *The Wizard of Oz*, for example, it was from Kansas that Dorothy and her dog 'Toto' were whisked away in a tornado and, according to the film, *My Fair Lady*, 'in Hertford, Hereford, and Hampshire, hurricanes hardly ever happen' so there's no real reason for the majority of us to panic. It does, though, sometimes happen that mini tornadoes and hurricanes occur in the quietest of places weather-wise and will pick up fallen leaves, old crisp packets and other assorted light debris and create a tiny yet intense, cyclone. Impossible to anticipate, if you happen to be out when one occurs, it's quite an exciting phenomena to observe.

STAR-GAZING

Even if it was broadcast way past their bedtime, granddads of a certain generation will have been brought up knowing of the monthly BBC television programme, *The Sky at Night* which (with only a couple of exceptions because of illness) was hosted by Patrick Moore from April 1957 until January 2013 – thus making it the longest-running programme with the same presenter in television history. Astonishing enough for that fact, even more remarkable is that it continues still with a different host (Patrick Moore having died in December 2012) and just shows the fascination that astronomy and star-gazing has for many people.

Some parts of the country make it easier to star-gaze than others. Light pollution over built-up areas sometimes prevents seeing the sky and stars clearly from the back garden but, elsewhere, on a clear night, it's possible to observe some of the 4,000 stars that twinkle in our universe all year round. Certain constellations are undoubtedly easier to recognize than others ('The Plough' and 'Orion's Belt', for instance) and in amongst them all, can often be glimpsed shooting stars and various satellites that orbit the earth.

On all but the warmest of summer nights, it can get quite cold out there so, when taking your grandchildren star-gazing, make sure they are wearing warm and suitable clothing. A drink and a bar of chocolate might also be a good idea! When star-gazing from a bedroom or back garden, a telescope is useful but otherwise, for the sake of mobility, a pair of binoculars will do the job just as well.

Those in the know advise that star-gazing is best done before the moon is full and suggest looking at the next new moon dates in order to work out the optimum times. However, star-gazing can (bearing in mind the light pollution and weather conditions) be done virtually anywhere and at any time – but particularly when camping and quite literally spending a night under the stars.

Periodically throughout the year, it is possible to watch meteor showers and, on a clear night, very impressive viewing they make! Travelling at 132,000 miles per hour, 500 times faster than the world's fastest car and 1,760 times quicker than a cheetah, these showers are caused by the debris from comets. Comets – described by one website as being 'dirty snowballs running around our solar system' – leave bits of dirt particles behind and our planet runs through many comet debris trails throughout the year. When Earth encounters these trails, the flecks of dirt strike our atmosphere and burn up to create a fascinating and quite beautiful natural light show.

When the various meteor showers are likely to occur, the media get quite excited and frequently mention the dates and times on TV, radio and in the social media – so you've no excuse for not knowing when the next one is likely to happen! If the weather is cloudy in your area, don't worry, as it might still be possible to watch them online.

CHAPTER 6: EXPLORE THE GREAT OUTDOORS

Any child that decides to take a particular activity more seriously and turn it into their chosen hobby or pastime is likely to need specialist equipment at some point. In the meantime, however, there are some items of general interest that will make excellent Christmas and birthday presents – just a few examples of which are listed below.

* Books on a particular activity

* Pond-dipping kits

* A cheap fishing rod or long-handled net for rock-pooling

* Small tent to camp in the garden – or to use as a den

* Basic digital camera

* Pair of binoculars

* Telescope – you can sometimes pick up telescopes quite cheaply at auctions or even on eBay

* Pen knife – every child loves the gift of a pen knife; as evidenced by this quote from Tom Sawyer written by Mark Twain in 1878: 'Mary gave him a bran-new "Barlow" knife worth twelve and a half cents; and the convulsion of delight that swept his system shook him to his foundations.'

Exploring the great outdoors may be as adrenalin pumping as described by Bear Grylls, Chief Scout, adventurer and television presenter who, in an interview, asked: 'When was the last time you explored the great outdoors? I mean really explored, when you set out into the unknown with a map and compass, a rucksack, a tent and sleeping bag; the sort of exploring that makes your heart beat faster.' Conversely, it may involve nothing more than a bus ride to a part of town never before visited.

Whatever its level of excitement and potential danger, of all the possible activities that a granddad and grandchildren can share, exploring in all its forms is arguably, the most important. As Richard Louv, American author and journalist put it; 'How can our kids really understand the moral complexities of being alive if they are not allowed to engage in those complexities outdoors?'

CAMPING

Modern materials and equipment may have taken some of the tent erecting skills out of camping but there's still a need to know where to pitch one's tent if there's any hope of avoiding a water-logged bed caused by overnight flash-flooding… location, location, location!

The website, 'Camping in the Forest' *(www.campingintheforest.co.uk)* suggests that it's well worth taking a few minutes to choose the best ground for your tent and to: 'Choose a spot on level, slightly soft ground, sheltered from the wind and with no hazards overhead such as trees or power lines. Pitch your tent with the back into the wind. Set up at least ten metres away from any open fires and barbecues in order to minimise the risk of sparks damaging the fabric.'

Further considerations might include of what exactly the ground consists. 'Ground is ground' you might think but, silly as it seems, some ground can be more comfortable than others – a fact you might wish you'd known when laying sleepless in the early hours.

Possibly the softest on which to sleep can be found in areas covered in pine needles, or even sand and dirt. As well as pitching a tent with its back to the wind, try and do so in the lee of a natural windbreak of a hedge and, if you are taking your grandchildren out during the hot summer months, be sure to pitch camp in a shaded area – tents in direct contact with the sun can get very hot indeed. Valleys at the bottom of hills often provide excellent tree cover and protection from the wind but, as mentioned at the outset, a sudden summer thunderstorm and deluge could mean that you are rudely awoken by a running cascade of water if you pitch your tent at the base of a gully. Lastly, whilst there is undoubtedly a certain romantic attraction to camping by the side of a stream or lake, less romantic is the fact that such areas are often frequented by midges and mosquitoes during a summer's evening – and there's nothing more such insects like than dining out on your blood!

Whether or not you've been driven out by swarms of biting insects, before leaving your campsite, always carry out a thorough check to ensure that you've left nothing behind. As the Country Code says: 'Take your litter home with you' – or at least to an appropriate rubbish bin. Most importantly, make sure any fire you have built is completely out and cold before leaving.

If a trip out into the wilds of the countryside is not possible, how about setting up camp in the back garden – and you don't even really need a tent, particularly if the grandchildren have a den or tree house out there. Some have successfully camped under or on a garden trampoline!

In a residential area, even with a lockable gate and reasonably secure panel fencing, there might be safety issues concerning leaving a child and their friends sleeping out in the garden with no adult present, so, much as 'Gramps' may well prefer the comfort of his own bed just a few feet away indoors, it will probably be best if he camps outside with them.

If there are real safety issues perhaps you could offer an alternative? What about letting them take over the sitting room for the night? They could have a tent in there or make a den out of chairs and sheets; throw cushions from the sofa on the floor and have a night with DVDs and normally forbidden treats until they fall asleep.

DIGGING UP THE PAST – JOIN IN WITH AN ARCHAEOLOGICAL DIG

The chances of digging up gold treasure are not as great as they once were but many happy hours can be spent by helpers on a site uncovering the contents of an ancient village rubbish dump and, in doing so, adding much to our knowledge of how our ancestors lived. Young and old love finding out about the past and there's something quite magical and awe-inspiring to touch something last handled several centuries ago and to stand where our ancestors stood Nothing beats the excitement of hands-on archaeology, and there are likely to be plenty of opportunities no matter where in the world you happen to live – you can't avoid history. You could even start an archaeological dig in the back garden and, if nothing is found, then you could turn the hole into a den – but that might not go down too well with parents or Grandma!

Various websites encourage volunteers and, for those as yet unsure about the suitability of archaeology for Granddad and his charges, point out that there is something for everyone; 'Young or old, fit or not, time rich or time poor…'

Other than in your own garden, it's perhaps as well not to carry out your own dig in what might be an archaeologically-sensitive area. Whilst little harm may be done with a little judicious digging, great care must however, be taken when contemplating running a metal detector over land which may be historically ancient. It is, in many instances, illegal to randomly metal detect in places of archeological interest unless under licence and even on less important agricultural land, metal detecting may be restricted or prohibited under the conditions of one of the Countryside Stewardship Schemes. With that in mind, should you be tempted to spend what would no doubt be an enjoyable hour or more in search of interesting objects, it is undoubtedly advisable to first of all seek permission from the landowner.

As well as helping out on a 'dig', another joint venture which might be equally enjoyed by granddads' and grandchildren is volunteering to work with one of the many conservation groups – even more opportunity to get muddy, play with water and have bonfires!

Certainly not confined to the countryside, activities include both urban and rural areas – and range from planting trees and wild flower meadows, to building stiles, clearing footpaths, coppicing, scrub clearance and fencing, dry-stone walling and helping to restore natural habitats along the coastline. No matter what or where, volunteer work helps ensures the future of the environment and, possibly most importantly, local wildlife.

Volunteering to lay a hedge is something that might appeal to some youngsters due to the opportunity to 'slash and burn' with a sharp bill-hook and a bonfire… and it is good exercise for Granddad too! You'll be in good company – HRH the Prince of Wales is an accomplished hedge-layer. The Council for the Protection of Rural England (CPRE) has an ongoing campaign to save British hedgerows and prevent the skill from becoming a dying art.

EXPLORE A BIG CITY (OR THE COUNTRYSIDE) ON A BUS

There's lots to do and see in a big city – and it need not be one never before visited on a mundane shopping trip for a new school uniform or other practical reasons. The High Street might be a road previously well-travelled by grandchildren but what about those normally off the beaten track? Where do they lead? What is at the end?

Both grandchildren and grandparents will most likely usually travel to town in a car. Despite the availability of a bus pass on his retirement, Granddad might not have been on such transport since his childhood and his grandchildren may never have done so. A bus ride is therefore, the basis for an exciting adventure, especially if it begins on the front seat at the top of a double-decker from where it's possible to look down on pedestrians and peer into people's back gardens whilst involuntary ducking as wayside overhanging branches clip the roof and scrape the side windows!

Big cities could already have organized sight-seeing buses from which to see the world and marvel at the famous buildings and statues but there's nothing to stop granddad from creating a city safari in any town. Even the most initially uninspiring place is likely to have a statue of interest to a child; quite often one that appertains to the area's business interest or past history – and what public conflict those might cause in these modern, extremely 'woke' days! Less controversially, there might be a monument in the shopping mall of a town built on the wool trade that shows an old shepherd, his dogs and sheep. A fishing port may display a monument to a famous sea rescue or influential individual; many of which, judging by the patina and shine, have obviously been clambered on and enjoyed by previous generations of children.

Museums and city galleries are a place for adventure and exploration whilst down quiet lanes and back streets of historical towns it is easy to fire the imagination of youngsters with tales (and, such is a grandfather's privilege, what is wrong with embroidering upon actual facts?!) of soldiers and smugglers.

In the manner of 'I-Spy' books, you should perhaps prepare a list of items likely to be seen on a city safari and tick each one off as it is noticed. They could be allocated points with the most likely to be observed earning one or two; the more unusual, ten points. Alternatively, the trip can be turned into a kind of treasure hunt with a list of things to 'collect' – perhaps taking photos of the things on your list and then creating a computer slideshow or hard-copy scrapbook.

While there's enjoyment to be had on a door-step safari within the local area, why not add a new dimension by encouraging country-based children to explore the city – and urban boys and girls to find things of interest in the country or, if a bus route from your local depot runs that far, the seaside? At the seaside, as well as finding interesting shells, seeking out fossils and exploring rock-pools, don't forget to sample traditional seaside fare such as cockles, mussels and candy floss!

FORAGING

Despite being common practice for generations and championed by the likes of Richard Mabey in the early 1970s, the idea of 'food for free' has, until relatively recently, been neglected. Nonetheless, these things go in cycles and foraging in the countryside is currently all the rage. Seeking out some of the naturally occurring crops and harvests of the countryside is a great opportunity for both granddad and grandchildren – provided it is done with care.

The different types of fungi come into season at different times of the year, but it is a traditional autumn treat to be out and about in the early morning. Only look in places where chemical fertilizers and sprays have not been used, as most types of spores will not tolerate such treatment. Carry a basket rather than a plastic bag in order to prevent damage to the mushrooms and, most importantly, make sure that you know without doubt exactly what you're picking.

Some types of fungi will only grow in certain types of soil; Morels, for example, prefer the edges of broad-leaved woodland, whereas the easily recognisable field mushrooms are found in open fields and meadows. In doing so, they confound the theory that mushrooms only grow well in damp, shady places.

As a source of wild herbs, the countryside cannot be bettered. If you know what you are looking for and the time of year you are most likely to find a particular herb, it should be possible to pick wild garlic, chives, fennel, horseradish and chervil (cow parsley). Some are definitely seasonal; wild garlic, for example, seen growing in many places, but particularly on the roadside banks of Cornwall, is only available during April/May time, whereas wild chives can be found almost all the year round.

Samphire can be bought, but it is obviously better if you can pick your own for nothing! Like sea spinach, it grows on estuaries below the high tide mark and can be eaten raw, or boiled and served with butter. Make traditional laver bread from the laver seaweed or chips from dulce; a reddish type of seaweed that grows along the northern coasts of the Atlantic and, in Northern Ireland, is a well-known snack food. From June to September, it is picked by hand at low tide and left out in the sun to dry before being either eaten as it is. It can also be pan-fried into chips or baked in the oven covered with cheese.

Sweet chestnuts grow wild in many places and as children like collecting things (and filling their pockets with 'treasures'), gathering them from the woodland floor during an early autumn walk is a fun thing to do. Stored, they can be brought out around Christmas-time and, as the song says, there's little better than 'chestnuts roasting on an open fire' at this time. Skinned, they can also be used as a traditional stuffing. Hazelnuts are common enough to find in the summer, as they are forming, but ripe ones not so easy in the autumn, due to the fact that squirrels and small mammals have generally got there before you!

In towns too, there are opportunities for foraging; scrubby wasteland can be a surprisingly good source of edible herbs and plants that have 'escaped' from urban gardens – and blackberries grow almost anywhere.

Care must, however, be taken. Whilst casual foraging is one thing, generally, it is likely to be illegal to totally uproot any wild plant. Some plants are more protected than others. Britain's *Wildlife & Countryside Act 1981*, for example, includes a periodically revised schedule of endangered plants protected against intentional picking, uprooting and destruction.

Whilst it all might sound quite draconian, it's actually all a matter of commonsense and those who wish to pick a few plants for pleasure, pursue botanical studies, collect specimens for educational purposes, or gather wild food for individual or family use are unlikely to feel the strong arm of the law! As a general rule:

*Only pick flowers and foliage from large patches of the plant

*Always pick in moderation

*Take care not to damage other vegetation unintentionally

FOSSIL COLLECTING AND BEACH-COMBING

Who has not wandered along a beach looking for shells and unusual beautiful stones as souvenirs which, in winter, turned in the palm of the hand, are an evocative reminder of summer days by the sea… and which parent or grandparent has not been made to carry a lump of driftwood by a child who has insisted on taking it home but is too tired to carry it?!

Originally, the expression 'beachcomber' came from a description of someone who actually earned a living by 'combing' the seashore in search of things to sell and trade but nowadays, the term can be applied to anybody who walks along the beach looking for anything interesting. What you are likely to find depends to some extent on the time of year; the storms of autumn and winter, for example, throw plenty of objects onto the seashore – ranging from crustaceans from the seabed to long ago discarded milk bottles and rusty tin-cans!

If the shore runs beneath a cliff made of soft rock or clay where the constant pounding of the waves at high tide have caused landslides and rock-falls, you might be lucky enough to discover some pieces of rock that contain fossils of ammonites (the relatives of modern-day two-shelled molluscs). If you are in an area known for fossils (the Jurassic Coast of south-west England, for instance), it could prove very worthwhile to split open any likely-looking small pieces of rock with the aid of a fossil hammer.

If you don't find a genuine dinosaur out fossil-collecting – then, rather than risk boredom setting in, combine beachcombing and fossil-hunting in order to build a pretend one out of any and every bit of available flotsam and jetsam, or out of piles of sand and pointy-shaped rocks. And if you can't even get to the beach, try fossil-hunting closer to home or have a dinosaur rally by making 'hobby-saurs' (like a broomstick hobby-horse, only scarier and with lots of teeth!) and giving a prize for the best/scariest one.

GEOCACHING

Granddad's childhood games meet new technology when it comes to geocaching! It's always been fun to follow a trail laid by others whether it be a paper one ('hare and hounds'), 'letter-boxing' (whereby clues in a story lead you to various landmarks), a treasure hunt following a list of (sometimes cryptic) clues, or in the somewhat complicated sport of 'orienteering' where various set places have to be reached by means of maps and a compass. Geocaching combines the lot… a treasure hunt for the digital generation, if you like. All you need is a handheld GPS, a pioneering spirit and enthusiasm. An outdoors activity, it is perhaps one of the most perfect for granddads' and their grandchildren and can be embarked upon wherever and whenever.

Basically, a geocache is a small waterproof box which has been hidden in woodland, fields, mountains, sea-front (anywhere in fact!) and has been given co-ordinates which can be downloaded via various apps.

But what's likely to be in the box once you've found it? It might be easier to ask what's *not* in the box as it seems most (small) objects have been included over the 20 years or so that geocaching has developed. The first ever was placed in America at the co-ordinates of 45°17.460′N 122°24.800′W and, according to *Wikipedia*, apparently held; 'software, videos, books, food, money, and a slingshot.'

More typically, today's boxes are likely to hold coins, ornamental buttons, small toys and similar objects – some of which are moved from cache to cache (with their whereabouts always being logged) and are known as 'hitch-hikers'. Generally, though, items are left, or can be swapped for others brought with you. If you take an item, you should always replace it with another. Each box also contains a log book (in which you can leave a message) and a pencil or pen. Happy geocaching!

RIDE BICYCLES AND EXPLORE NEW PLACES

Getting out and about on bikes is an excellent joint activity and introducing your grandchild to the joy and excitement of cycling is one of the thrills of being a granddad. Yes, there'll be tears and tantrums – and cries of 'I can't do it' as a child fails to turn the corner, wobbles and ends up a crumpled heap on the floor but, irrespective of these little setbacks, it's well worth all the effort!

The garden path or lawn isn't necessarily the best place to learn as, although they may have a relatively smooth surface, there are all too often the confines of wall corners, limited space (and potential damage to the prize flowerbeds) to consider. Instead, if there's a quiet piece of road or car park where the tyro rider is not likely to crash into someone's cherished Rolls Royce, begin the lessons there. Best of all, however, is a nearby park or children's playground with plenty of space.

Start by helping them get to learn to balance on a small bike. Teach them how to push themselves off but keeping feet just a little above the ground and not on the pedals. Keep doing it until they get used to balancing – and only then introduce the concept of using the pedals and brakes. Building up confidence is all-important at this stage. Encourage them to look ahead, not at the ground or at you. Finally, practice going round those dreaded corners – one way to do this is to get them to chase 'Gramps', but he should always remember to run in wide circles!

Once competent, there's a whole new world out there. You could, for instance, try your hand at bicycle polo; obstacle courses, orienteering and trail-riding – or you could, of course, just take yourselves off for a gentle spin!

There are plenty of models of bicycles to choose from and, although the more elderly of the party might prefer the ease of an electric bike, traditionally, if you intend eventually going out into the countryside together and tackling those muddy tracks and woodland paths, a robust

BMX or mountain bike type will probably be favourite but it really does all depend on whether you are going off-road, down to the shops, or attempting to qualify for the next Tour de France. Ask at your local bike shop if you're unsure – almost all will be happy to offer help and advice.

In order for children to learn responsibility for their possessions, it's not a bad idea to teach them how to repair and maintain their bicycles; doing so provides yet another perfect opportunity for a granddad/grandchild bonding session. In addition, children also learn various physical and educational skills such as physics, mechanics, maths and the functions of various tools.

TRACKING IN THE SNOW, SAND AND MUD

There are many exciting things about a fresh fall of snow: snowball fights, sledging and snowman-building being the obvious ones. But before rushing about and contaminating the pristine covering with human footprints, it can be both fun and educational to discover what wildlife has been there ahead of you.

Possibly not all that dangerous unless in the wild country of America or forests of Canada, even without the chance of bumping into a mountain lion or grizzly bear, this can still be quite exciting as you track a fox (or the neighbour's cat) across the garden. Further afield, it might be possible to identify the paw prints of badgers (looking like those of a miniature bear) or the slots of deer or wild boar crossing a field or woodland ride.

It's actually not necessary to wait for a snowfall either: one of the great things about ditches or pond edges is that there are, at most times of the year, usually the odd muddy patch to be found somewhere along their length – and these are wonderful places to play 'nature detective'. Any clear damp area will often show the footprints of birds and animals and it is surprising just how much evidence of different species one can glean, even though you might rarely see the bird or beast that created them.

Look out for any worn crossing points as it is quite likely they are made by deer or hares, the prints of which can often be easily seen. With experience, it is even possible to work out the individual deer species; roe have smaller, more closed hoof prints than do say, a fallow deer. Evidence of webbed feet will suggest wild duck – most likely mallard – and sprawled-out bird prints with just a touch of 'webbing' between them, either coots or moorhens. Pheasants like marshy areas and their chicken-like footprints are easy to spot. As otters are now known to frequent every county of the UK, it might even be possible to see their footprints in the mud. However, it is probably more likely that they were made by mink. The mink's pad-marks are smaller than otters' but, unless you have the two to compare, how can you tell?! Notes, sketches and photographs will help in any 'identification parade' once you get home and have access to both the internet and any reference books.

Another option might be to make a plaster cast of an animal's footprint. It's a relatively easy thing to do and just requires plaster of Paris (which used to be available from most chemists but nowadays more likely art/craft shops, decorator's merchants or online), water, a small bucket in which to mix it (plus a stick for mixing), a strip of pliable cardboard (the type used to support packaged men's shirts when new is perfect) and a couple of paper clips.
* Make a 'collar' of cardboard wide enough in circumference to surround the animal track to be cast – and hold it in a circle with the two paper clips.
* Wearing gloves and taking great care not to get the fine dry powder in your eyes, mix the plaster of Paris (at a rate of two parts to one part of water) and very carefully pour it into the collar of cardboard.
* Within ten minutes or so, it will have set and the plaster cast can be lifted from the ground – and should contain a perfect paw print on the underside. Leave it natural or paint the cast once back at home and before adding it to your collection of 'interesting things'!
NB: Take great care as the plaster of Paris sets and never touch it with bare fingers – the chemical reaction caused by the addition of water can generate a great amount of heat.

In the absence of any animal tracks to follow, why not track Granddad across the snow, mud or sandy beach?! Given a few minutes 'law', his foot prints can then be followed by his pursuers. A clever 'Gramps' can make things difficult by running several times round a tree or large rock, walking backwards to confuse his hunters and jumping across any narrow ditches and then re-crossing further 'up-stream'!

VISIT A MUSEUM OR ART GALLERY

Danger doesn't always have to be experienced by the participants of a day out. Quite often it is enough for youngsters to learn of the perils and dangers experienced by others in times gone by and, with this in mind, a museum or gallery is an excellent place to visit. Sadly, too few people take children to either, at least according to a survey which suggested that; 'Kids are more likely to recognise a McDonalds than Madame Tussaud's…[and] are just as likely to be ignorant of well-known artists such as Monet, Rembrandt, Van Gogh or Picasso – unless covering them in the school syllabus.'

It looks like granddad's everywhere may have their work cut out, but a few trips during the year to museums, art galleries and landmarks will prove to be memorable, informative and fun occasions for youngsters, particularly on a wet day.

Some pre-planning might be in order – either research on the internet or visit the destination first before embarking on your museum-based adventure. Choose the intended venue carefully as some places are more child-friendly than others, and some exhibits are more likely to engage than others. If a temporary exhibition is known to be popular, try to visit early or late in the day so as to avoid the worst of the crowds and, if it can be done without incurring the wrath of the attendants (many museums and galleries have strict rules about food and drink in the exhibition halls), take some drinks and snacks, so you can instantly prevent any demands for food that may otherwise necessitate finding the café and queuing.

Never stay too long with very young children; it's better to leave on a high than once they've got bored. Finally, have crayons, pencils and a drawing pad with you and ignore any pleas to be allowed to take photos on your mobile phone of any exhibits and paintings that may have caught their eye. Instead, encourage them to sit and have a go at their own artwork: who knows what masterpieces they will create – just don't let them try and graffiti those hanging on the wall!

<u>CHAPTER 7: FISHING FOR FUN</u>

Fishing allows that extra step from pond dipping for tadpoles and sticklebacks – and what can be more traditional a pastime than a grandparent taking their grandchildren for a day out at the water's edge? Encouraging youngsters into any such activity is not only good for the future well-being of fishing, it is good for the well-being of the child as it encourages exercise and facilitates learning about the flora and fauna.

Whilst the first time is always a big, exciting adventure, it depends on how the day is approached and planned as to whether the enthusiasm lasts long enough for a second trip out. It will if you bear a few elementary 'rules' in mind.

Granddad needs to 'mug-up' about fishing and, unless taking lessons from a professional, has to have at least some of the answers to the inevitable questions! Encourage and praise and – particularly when fly-fishing – include several breaks for a drink and a snack, or even just for a little wander along the bankside to see what there might be of general interest. Insects hatching, damsel and dragonflies skimming over the water, frogs, tadpoles, a moorhen's nest and a flock of sheep grazing in the next field are all fascinating additions to the actual job in hand.

Whether it be coarse fishing or fly-fishing depends on several factors; just three of which are availability, accessibility and cost. There is undoubtedly more finesse required for fly-fishing, but there is also action – whereas with coarse fishing there are inevitably, long periods of inactivity when all that's required is to sit quietly and watch your float bobbing in the water. Peaceful though it might be, doing so could get boring for a youngster.

In the UK, every person of twelve and over should have a rod licence before going fishing. They can be obtained from post offices and also purchased on line by visiting the relevant Environment Agency website. On the same website can be found fishing guides containing lists of waters where fishing is allowed – and the methods permitted. Local fishing tackle shops can also help.

Until the continued enthusiasm is guaranteed there is no need to buy expensive equipment and for coarse fishing its best to keep things simple at first. The experts advise using a short spinning rod which can easily be handled by a young person and fitting it with a fixed-spool reel which are very easy for a youngster to use. It is, however, important that the young angler has some input into the choice of equipment in order that they feel completely involved. Chances are they will select the largest and brightest float in the shop.... the kind of float that is designed to warn ships of shallow water!

There are inevitable dangers associated with both coarse and fly-fishing but with the latter, not only are you close to water (sometimes very deep water), you are casting with a sharp hook at the end of a very long fly-line and, for these reasons alone, a child should be made aware of these potential hazards. In addition, it is necessary to be able to concentrate and because of the need to be almost constantly casting, it can be very tiring so an individual needs to be sufficiently developed both mentally and physically.

With that in mind, there is, fortunately, a huge selection of fishing equipment specifically geared toward the younger angler. It is important that the rod length is easily manageable as, not only is there the physical aspect to consider, the right length and weight ensures that they can 'feel' the rod and line as they cast.

You can of course buy the standard range of artificial flies from tackle dealers, but they are expensive – especially if you keep losing them as they become entangled in the tree branches during a tricky back-cast! Tying your own flies might become a hobby in itself – and there's the added delight and satisfaction of raising a trout to an imitation fly of your own design and manufacture. The basic tools that you will need are: a fly-tying vice, some hackle-pliers, an assortment of hooks, material with which to create your flies (feathers, fur, chenille, etcetera) tying threads and, most importantly, one of the many available books showing the dressings and 'how-to' methods of the most popular patterns.

'Tickling' trout is a traditional countryside pastime – with varying degrees of success. Wikipedia has much of interest to say on the subject – and includes an extract taken from Thomas Martindale's 1901 book, *Sport Indeed*. It describes the method perfectly:

'The fish are watched working their way up the shallows and rapids. When they come to the shelter of a ledge or a rock it is their nature to slide under it and rest. The poacher sees the edge of a fin or the moving tail, or maybe he sees neither; instinct, however, tells him a fish ought to be there, so he takes the water very slowly and carefully and stands up near the spot. He then kneels on one knee and passes his hand, turned with fingers up, deftly under the rock until it comes in contact with the fish's tail. Then he begins tickling with his forefinger, gradually running his hand along the fish's belly further and further toward the head until it is under the gills. Then comes a quick grasp, a struggle, and the prize is wrenched out of his natural element, stunned with a blow on the head, and landed in the pocket of the poacher.'

For fun, rather more than practicality, you could try making your own fishing equipment either at home or whilst out on the riverbank. All that's needed is a reasonably straight, reasonably strong yet 'whippy' stick or branch, a length of line or string, a float of some description and a hook fashioned from a safety pin, small nail or short piece of strong wire which has been bent into a rough hook shape and pointed.

Something like bamboo from the garden or hazel or willow from the woods form the basis of a good rod and it should be cut to the same length (or just a little more) as the height of the person for whom it is being made. Cut off all the branch nodules and, to the thinnest end, attach a piece of thin string or fishing line cut slightly longer than the rod.

Thread the line through a previously drilled hole running through the centre of an old wine cork or, if out in the wilds, construct a float out of any piece of tree bark or a nutshell that is large enough to keep your string, hook and bait afloat (you will need to make a hole in order to run your string or length of line through it) and make sure that there is the right amount of line left below the float so that the baited hook doesn't drag into the pond or stream bed. Once you've decided where the float needs to be, tie a knot in the line above and below it, so that it is kept in place. To the loose end, fix your hook (it needs to be bent with an 'eye' shaped at the top and a point at the bottom). Next comes the gruesome bit (and yet the part which all young children love!). Dig around until you find a worm – or if you can't find a worm, seek out a grub or caterpillar from the surrounding vegetation – and attach it to your hook.

Begin fishing by casting the line into the water… and wait a while. When you see the float move, swiftly lift upwards and backwards. Hopefully a fish will have attached itself and you can gently tease it to the bankside. Unless you've managed to catch a trout of decent size, carefully remove the hook from the fish's mouth, admire it, photograph it and then return it sensitively to the water.

GO CRABBING

Whilst out and about at the seaside or near an estuary, it's easy enough to incorporate a spot of crabbing into the adventure. There's very little equipment needed; just a piece of string, bait and possibly a small weight of some description. A fishing net (such as those sold alongside the traditional bucket and spade at a seaside shop) might also be useful so that you can place it under the caught crab just before lifting it from the water.

With a strong instinct for self-preservation, crabs tuck themselves away in areas of water where they are safe under the cover of rocks, seaweed, or places around the base of a pier or harbour wall. They can, though, be enticed out by the correct bait!

Apparently, crabs seek their food by smell rather than sight and the fresher the bait the better. Quite what you use is down to personal preference but many traditionalists think bacon pieces to be the best. Other possibilities are slivers of chicken or fish but one particular website recommends the use of frozen sand eels bought from the local sea fishing bait shop. Another site advises frequent changing of bait ('every three-four pulls') and makes the very valid point that it makes no sense to throw the discarded bait into the water as, if you do, you're just giving crabs more dining opportunities.

Having securely attached your bait (and weight if the bait is too light to properly sink) to the string, drop it into the water and let it rest at the bottom. With the string loosely between your fingers, you should be able to feel when a crab starts nibbling at his free meal on the other end. Now is the time for a little skill to come into play – if you think he's got a firm bite on the bait, start slowly bringing up the line and avoid any jerky movements. You'll very likely lose a few before you get the hang of it but 'practice makes perfect'!

The crabs you catch will probably be too small for the table but, with this type of fishing, it's more about having fun, and is a great way of learning about some of the seaside's most interesting creatures. Bearing in mind their universal love of collecting, most children like to amass the caught crabs and for this reason, a bucket filled with seawater and containing a few pebbles or lump of seaweed under which they can hide, will keep the crabs safe and content until they can all be gently released back into the water at the end of the session.

CHAPTER 8: HIGH FLYERS – TAKE TO THE AIR!

Even as grandparents, despite having sat through various school lessons and watched programmes on television, how a heavy aeroplane manages to fly in the sky is still a source of wonderment to many of us! No wonder then, children find things that whizz through the air, equally as mystifying … and fascinating.

In our own childhood, which of us did not play with those balsa-wood gliders that could loop and glide both indoors and outside, or with paper 'darts' whenever the teacher's back was turned! Remote-controlled planes, kites of all descriptions, and even a boomerang that may or may not return to its handler, all continue to intrigue both young and old alike. In fact, most granddads are still big kids at heart and, the bigger the kid, the bigger and better is the toy with which he likes to play!

When it comes to throwing a boomerang, there's a definite skill required! On a children's playing field recently, I was told by a little boy that his boomerang had 'come back two times' but that his daddy's one 'hadn't come back at all and is stuck up a tree'!

Where 'Dad' might have gone wrong could have been for one of several reasons. The art of throwing a boomerang and getting it to return – the latter being the most difficult bit! – has to do with wind, how it's being held and the angle at which it is being thrown.

Throwing out in a field or park is a good idea – and not just because of the safety aspect. In a typical suburban garden surrounded by houses, any wind there may be is forced downwards by the buildings whereas, in an open field or playing ground, there is more of a chance of throwing into, or more accurately, 'around' an upward, undisturbed wind. Different boomerangs require throwing at different angles but generally, the experts suggest starting by throwing the boomerang at a 45-50 degree angle to the right of the wind and experimenting from there.

How you hold a boomerang prior to lift-off is important, as is the height of your throw when you release it. The curved edge should be facing you and, accepting that you've mastered the angle at which to launch it into the wind, most types work best when released at eye-height. If there are any mature trees or roof tops in the distance, aim for the tops of these and pray that it turns to come home before it gets caught up there! As to that all-important grip, use a pinching method and hold the wing between forefinger and thumb.

According to one particular website – and it's an Australian one so they should know! – 'imparting spin to the departing boomerang is crucial… Don't "let go" of the boomerang; let it rip its way out of your hand.'

Yet another emphasizes the need for some nifty footwork; 'When you're getting ready to throw, turn your right foot out and pick your left foot up, balancing on your right foot. Step forward with your left foot at the same time you throw…'

With so much technicality involved, it is quite surprising that boomerang-throwing isn't an Olympic sport – but just think of the satisfaction achieved when it returns to hand like a well-trained homing pigeon. When it does, hold your nerve and don't be tempted to run away. Instead, take a side step and let it past or, if it's lost speed and momentum, impress your audience by catching it at chest level between the palms of your hands.

GROUND CONTROL TO MAJOR TOM!

Balsa-wood gliders were likely to be Granddad's only option 'back in the day'; nowadays, however, with the relative cheapness and easy availability of radio-controlled helicopters, planes, and even drones, things are very different.

Flying UAVs (unmanned aerial vehicles) can be great fun – and also potentially dangerous. For this reason, things that fly by remote control are often restricted by local by-laws or owners of land to which the public have access. Quite rightly some might say: imagine the confusion of a dog-walker for instance, who, when hearing a panicked called to 'Duck!' looks up expecting to see nothing more than a feathered water bird and is instead, faced by a miniature helicopter hurtling towards them.

Public parks might not, therefore, be the best place to begin your aviation career; even Granddad's old-fashioned glider can come down quite heavily on a picnic plate of sandwiches and will not endear you to the participants. Try and find an area of private land – a local farmer might not object if asked whether you can use a corner of a field not currently growing a harvestable crop and is well away from livestock… and, if permission is granted, the odd bottle of wine or whiskey should go a long way towards ensuring that permission will continue!

The mechanics of flying radio-controlled UAVs notwithstanding, a couple of tips as to getting the best from a balsa wood model might not come amiss:
* A steady, smooth, level throw – propelling it too hard will only result in it looping towards *terra-firma*; the aim is to establish a steady glide (done correctly, it's possible to achieve glides of a minute or much longer, especially if one hits a thermal)
* Flight is also dependent on both the plane's centre of gravity and the angle of the horizontal part of the tail – adjust the centre of gravity by adding or removing modelling clay or Blu-Tack on the nose, and the angle of the tail by gently bending or warping (with water).

KITES IN THE SKY

Apparently, in China, kite festivals and even a designated 'Kites' Day' have long been occasions for everyone – men, women and children – to go kite-flying. Traditionally, these were made in the form of birds that flap their wings, snakes that sway and swoop, and insects that buzz. Now, I'm not suggesting that you attempt anything anywhere near as complicated but there's no reason why you shouldn't have an equal amount of fun with a simple kite that is easy to build and, given the right weather conditions, easy to fly.

Such kites may be anywhere between 30cm (1ft) and 90cm (3ft) high. The frame is made from two light garden canes, a shorter one crossing a longer vertical one just above its centre. At the crossing point the canes should be lashed together with string or, probably easiest, with binding tape. A length of string is then tied to the top of the cross and stretched around the frame, passing through notches cut into the end of each cane. The string is then tightly and securely tied at the point at which you started (the top of the cross).

Cover the frame with strong paper, thin fabric or even the plastic of a black dustbin liner; secure it by sticking, sewing or taping it over the string edges (*NB*: This cover should be cut 2.54cm (1in) larger than the frame and shouldn't be stretched too tightly.) Next, fasten a slack string between the ends of the shorter length of cane and another to each end of the longer cane. At their crossing point, tie the towing line (the length of which depends on how high in the sky you think your kite might eventually fly!).

A tail, made from bits of paper tied onto another length of string (the paper should look like several bow-ties tied at spaces along the tail's length) is fastened to the base of the kite around the bottom of the longest cane. Once in flight, if the kite continually dives, adjust the length of the tail according to the weight of the kite.

Generally, and contrary to popular opinion, the top of a hill is not necessarily the best place to fly a kite; while a reasonable breeze is required, too gusty a wind might break it. A flat field or children's play area, well away from trees and overhead wires is the easier place to try or, if you are near enough, the beach is perfect.

Of course, it's possible to buy cheap kites – or even expensive ones that their manufacturers claim will perform all manner of exciting tricks – but whatever type you choose, there's always that sense of exhilaration once your kite is air-borne; a thrill experienced by all kite flyers through the generations.

ZIP, ZIP, ZIPPING ALONG!

For some inexplicable reason, very young children like to make their toys do the most horrendous things – and throwing a doll or similar through the air in order to make them 'fly' causes great delight and a huge amount of laughter. Attaching a string to the middle of one of them – a toy, not the child! – and sending it whizzing down a clothesline in the manner of a miniature zip-wire can have the same effect… or maybe it's just the children I know that do these sorts of things?!

Assuming that it's not, I'm sure that even more excitement will occur if one is able to create a temporary zip-wire capable of carrying the weight of a child aged around five to nine years of age (it's my experience that children above nine become real sensation-seekers and a mild ride across the garden just will not do).

A long stretch of garden isn't always necessary – a zip-wire of only 20 metres (21yds) with a sloping fall of around 1 metre (39in) from start to end point should be sufficient to produce enough of an adrenalin rush for the rider (and possibly also their doll or stuffed toy!) If your garden slopes, so much the better but even if it doesn't, the angle/speed of the zip-wire can be set by the height of the starting point.

For a temporary zip-wire, if you are using trees as your anchor points, make sure that the bark is protected from damage by the zip-wire itself by inserting padding between the tree and whatever you are using as the 'cable'. Without the convenience of trees, it might be possible to securely fasten a tethering ring to the house wall or even, for very young children, use the points between two substantially fixed washing line posts. Concrete posts such as are used to erect panel fencing might be another option – just don't blame me if your child charge subsequently crashes through the panelling and into next-door's garden!

CHAPTER 9: HUBBLE, BUBBLE, TOIL AND TROUBLE – COOK SOMETHING!

Taking advantage of a rainy day in order to learn and cook some staple recipes is never a bad idea. However, more unusual and exciting might be the possibility of slaving over a hot stove in order to create scary Halloween dishes at the appropriate time of year. Likewise, much can be made from ingredients that may have been collected during a foraging expedition; particularly if the ingredients have a certain 'yuck' factor!

Nettles would probably come into the above category and yet they can make good soup if the young shoots are chosen – and incorporate a certain element in their picking if you don't want to get stung!

In the spring or whenever young nettle leaves can be found, carefully pick 500g (wear gloves) from a site unlikely to be contaminated by car exhaust fumes, farm sprays or your neighbour's dog! Back in the kitchen, bring a large pot of water to the boil and add two teaspoons of salt. Drop in the nettles, and cook for between one and two minutes until they begin to soften. Drain them in a colander before rinsing them off in cold water.

Heat one tablespoon of olive oil in a saucepan over medium-low heat, and stir a skinned chopped and diced onion. Cook until the onion has softened and turned translucent (about five minutes) and then stir in four tablespoons of basmati rice, one litre of chicken stock and the nettles. Bring all to the boil before reducing the heat to medium-low. Cover and simmer until the rice is tender (approximately 15 minutes). Puree the soup with an immersion blender, and season to taste with salt and pepper.

Blackberries and other hedgerow fruits make tasty jams and chutneys –but some methods of jam-making can be quite complicated, requiring jam thermometers, preserving pans, straining kits and jelly bags. This method is so much simpler and can be used to make big batches to store for Christmas giving, or in small amounts for immediate use. There is no complicated weighing either – all you need to do is remember to weigh out twice as many blackberries to sugar before placing both into a suitably-sized pan. Next add a couple of tablespoons of lemon juice and bring to the boil. Immediately it has, lessen the heat and simmer (without stirring) for 20 minutes. Take a teaspoon of the preserve from the mix and place it on a saucer; put the saucer in the fridge for five minutes during which time it should set – if it doesn't, keep cooking and testing every five minutes until it does. Finally, if you are intending storing your jam, pour or spoon it into clean sterilized jars and screw the lids on tightly.

CAMPFIRE COOKING

In an interview, Bear Grylls, Chief Scout, explorer and adventurer recalled that, as a child, he was once given one match and one raw sausage and was told to go and cook it: 'I remember looking at the match and looking at the sausage and thinking, it's going to have to burn for a very long time! Then someone showed me how to make a fire…'

Just to be on the safe side, it may pay to take dry sticks and newspapers for lighting the fire with you. Hunting for suitable dry kindling, while exciting for the first few minutes soon palls if all that can be found is damp after a rainy time the evening before. Damp sticks are though, okay to fuel the fire once it is properly going but ideally, use well-dried, well-seasoned wood. Ash burns particularly well, as will oak if cut or broken into small enough pieces. Some woods spit more than others so watch out for children's safety. For this reason, don't be tempted into using pine – which could also taint any meat you might be cooking because of its turpentine type smell.

It is a good fire-base that ensures the success or otherwise of a campfire meal – cooking over an open flame only gives raw meat a singed surface, whereas charcoal burning grey, but shot with a reddish glow will give a constant heat. Get your fire going well in advance of when you are likely to need it – there's nothing worse than an impatient, fractious and hungry child! Depending on the wind conditions and the likely draught, an hour ahead is not too early. Low heat can be gained by spacing out the charcoal and a hot one by flicking away the white ash from the top of the burning wood. Charcoal – and one little tip from my Boy Scout days; always add fuel from the edge of the fire rather than piling it directly on top.

Making baked bean can pancakes

Ingenious and fun, this method of campfire cooking requires a little preparation – and a large empty baked bean can (although any tin can will do). Having taken off one end of the can in order to remove the contents, towards the end that is left, spear a ring of small holes around the side in order to allow air flow.

Make a pancake batter from one egg, about two ounces (57g) plain flour and approximately half a pint (150ml) of milk. Add a pinch of salt and mix the batter until smooth and free of any lumps.

Carefully put the upturned tin in the embers of the fire and once it has warmed through (it won't take long), drizzle a drop of cooking oil or smear of butter on to the top and gently add a spoonful of your batter mix. There should be no need to turn the resultant pancake as, restricted in depth by the rim of the baked bean can, they'll be thin enough to have cooked right through.

A variation on this can be tried at home in the following way. Take your empty tin and make air-holes in it as described above. Then cut a square access hole in the front of the tin – use tin-snips to cut a square from the open end of the tin. Place the tin can 'cooker' over a couple of lit candles. 'Tea-lights' work well but make certain that the candles and tin can cooker are stable before beginning your pancake-making.

Making 'damper' bread

Why not cook 'Dampers' (a type of bread) over a campfire by wrapping the dough around a hazel stick or similar pared down to skewer-shape with the aid of your trusty pen-knife? Most granddads' will have made these at cub or scout camp!

All you need to make a couple of dampers is one cup of self-raising flour, a teaspoon of sugar, a pinch of salt, a tablespoon of butter and about half a cup of milk. Rub the butter into the flour until it has a crumb-like consistency and then add in the sugar and salt before slowly adding the milk and stirring it in until a dough is formed. Divide the mixture into two and roll each into a long thin sausage-shape before twisting it around your stick skewer (the way the dough is wrapped around the stick explains the damper's other name of 'twisters'). Some add a few raisins to the mix but whether you do or not, the dampers are then baked slowly over the hot embers of the campfire. Take care to only use the embers, as if you cook over the flames you will end up with blackened bread on the outside and a raw lump of dough in the centre!

As with the damper, if you try and bake a potato in the middle of the campfire, all that will happen is that you'll have a burnt and very undercooked potato. Instead, the recipe for success is to pull some hot embers from the campfire and cook in those.

Cut your potatoes lengthways and add a knob of butter (which helps prevent the potato from drying out as it cooks) before wrapping them tightly in tin foil. Making sure you have enough embers to do so, 'bury' the potatoes in the glowing coal or charcoal so they are covered both top and bottom. Depending on their size, they could take as long as three-quarters of an hour to cook so now is the time to go off and do something useful! Test to see if they are ready by (carefully – you don't want to burn yourself) pushing a finger into the side of the wrapped potato. If it feels soft and your finger leaves a dent, it's ready!

A WINTER PICNIC

Way back in 1966, when some who are granddads' now may have been just children themselves, Penguin books published *Something to Do*, by 'Septima'. In it, they included the idea of a winter picnic, but advised the reader to 'Wait for the right day. One of those fine, clear, bright winter days, when everything looks and feels sharper than usual' before setting off, 'very warmly wrapped up, to the nearest open space.'

Such a trip on such a day weather-wise sounds just as attractive now as it did then. Food for a winter picnic is, however, likely to be somewhat different to that suggested for the summer and, instead of sandwiches and a cold drink, an insulated picnic bag containing warmed Cornish pasties, pies, potatoes baked in their jackets and thermos flasks of soup, stew, hot chocolate or blackcurrant juice may be that much more appropriate.

CHAPTER 10: LIKE A DUCK TO WATER

'Row, row, row your boat,

Gently down the stream.

Merrily, merrily, merrily, merrily,

Life is but a dream.'

Where better to spend a warm summer's day than by the water's edge? Like fire, most children and adults find water irresistible. It's a medium in which to play, enjoy a sport and learn about all things aquatic. It is, though, potentially dangerous – and, irrespective of this book's title, not necessarily in a good way – so must be must be treated with great care and respect.

Where opportunity allows, canoeing and/or kayaking is a great adventure for sensation-seeking granddads and their grandchildren. Probably the best way to begin is by taking lessons at a sports centre or canoe club – of which there are several in the US, the UK and throughout Europe. Once competent (and certain that the children in your charge want to continue with the activity), it may be time to contemplate a canoe of your own and exploring the ponds, rivers and wide streams in your area.

Paddling skills and an understanding of how to manage weight and boat balance are critical. As the European Child Safety Alliance point out: 'A capsize is just as likely to occur in calm water as in rough water.' They go on to mention the fact that most capsizes occur by the 'casting of a fishing rod, by leaning over to retrieve something out of the water, horseplay, or standing to change positions or relieve oneself.' Both granddad and his grandchildren do, therefore, need to know exactly how to behave in the event of a capsize as well as being able to regain control of the canoe and re-enter it from the water.

Having said all that, canoeing and kayaking is an excellent way of exploring otherwise inaccessible places, getting close to wildlife (animals and birds are far less wary of people in a canoe than they are of those on foot on dry land) and learning about the water's ecosystem. It's also very good exercise!

DAM A STREAM LIKE A BEAVER!

Simple, yet very fulfilling and satisfying, I can't think of any child (or adult) that doesn't get pleasure from damming a stream or temporarily altering a watercourse! Maybe it has something to do with harnessing the force of nature in some small way, but the fact remains that it is a very pleasurable activity and can be done in order to create a pool on which to sail a model boat, or simply as a way of whiling away the hours dabbling in water with naturally occurring stones, small boulders and logs.

On a warm summer's day, provided that one can be sure the stream or riverbed is unlikely to contain broken glass or sharp objects, it can be carried out with bare feet and in shorts but at other times, Wellingtons are definitely a good idea – despite the fact that there is a good chance that they might be full of water by the end of the day!

You do need to exercise a certain degree of responsibility, though. As well as the obvious dangers of messing about in water, you should always make sure that the dam is deconstructed before you leave. It might be fun to see what effect your dam has had some 24 hours later but water blocked where it shouldn't be can have far-reaching effects on the immediate environment and its flora and fauna.

POND-DIPPING AND ROCK-POOLING

A small area of shallow water is undoubtedly the perfect place for children to paddle about in their wellingtons' armed with just a stick, a net and a jam-jar or, for a more technical approach, one of the many pond-dipping kits available. Depending on their contents, the price of these kits are generally affordable enough to make a relatively inexpensive birthday or Christmas present – and, perhaps more importantly, be the first step in encouraging and enthusing the nature-lovers, biologists and botanists of the future.

Typically, a pond-dipping kit might include a net on a handle, sampling pots, a magnifying bug pot with a measurement grid on its base, a small sampling tray and plastic pipette. Most also contain an identification booklet or laminated waterproof chart.

Once collected and identified, children can even create their own 'bucket zoo', and then give friends and family a guided tour – after which the exhibits should be returned to from whence they came.

RAFT RACING
Huckleberry Finn punted one up the backwaters of the Mississippi and Thor Heyerdahl famously sailed one across the Pacific Ocean.

Rafts of all shapes and sizes have fascinated many and, provided that you are not intending to take one on too perilous a journey, are quite easy to construct in the back garden. Getting it to a suitable stretch of water may, however, be a different matter. Nevertheless, it's a project that could be worth the effort as there are many raft-races held during the summer months – several of which are organised in aid of charity. Building your raft and competing with it at such events helps others and, should your raft prove not all that 'sea-worthy' at least there will be trained rescuers at hand!

Most rafts are constructed using four, or possibly more, plastic barrels as buoyancy (the number depends on the size), around which a wooden frame is built to provide parallel and cross-supports. Fixing the frame securely round the barrels can be done using bolts, screws, nails or even rope but remember that, if the buoyancy aids are drilled into for easy fixing, there's a good chance of water seeping in through any of the holes thus made. Prevent this by ensuring that the drum lids are watertight and that any holes are plugged with plumber's glue or sealant.

Whilst 'go-faster' stripes painted along the side of your raft will not help with speed, anything that makes the front of the vessel more like the prow, rather than the stern of a boat will assist when propelling it through the water. You could add a rudder or alternatively (and dependent on how many are intended to 'man' your raft), the two back oarsmen can use their paddles in order to steer. Depending on your design – but from experience, it seems that most rafts evolve rather than are constructed from plans – you might also like to attach a plywood deck and even add seating of some kind. Rafting aficionados offer further advice in the shape of the following tips and observations:
* Lighter rafts are faster – but become more unstable, particularly if the crew outweigh the craft.
* The lower the centre of gravity, the more stable the craft, but the less amount of barrel in the water, the faster it will go because there is less 'drag'.

CHAPTER 11: WHITTLE WHILE YOU WORK!

'Whittling' – the dictionary definition being to:

'Cut or pare thin shavings from (wood) with a knife

Make or fashion (an object) in this manner.'

Whittling is often seen as being a somewhat old-fashioned pastime; and one particularly favoured by the hobos' of America during the late 19th century – as evidenced by Mark Twain, writing in, *The Adventures of Huckleberry Finn*:

'All the stores was along one street. They had white domestic awnings in front, and the country-people hitched their horses to the awning-posts. There was empty dry-goods boxes under the awnings, and loafers roosting on them all day long, whittling them with their Barlow knives; and chawing tobacco, and gaping and yawning and stretching – a mighty ornery lot.'

Whether any of today's generation of granddads' could be considered a 'mighty ornery lot' is not for me to say but it is, however, a pretty safe bet that they will, in their childhood, have no doubt indulged in a bit of whittling of one sort or another. Perhaps now is the time to teach this rapidly disappearing pastime to their grandchildren?

Part of the reason for its decline is, of course, the general modern attitude towards penknives. A few decades back, almost every boy would have had such a knife in his pocket – and how many mothers cursed the fact when it got left there and only reappeared as it rattled round the washing machine drum whenever a muddy pair of jeans were washed!). Nowadays however, to be found with a penknife in one's pocket for no real reason leaves its owner open to the accusation of having suspicious motives.

With only innocent intent, it's necessary to start with a good quality knife, by which is meant one with a good quality steel blade. Whilst there are many options available, some are quite expensive and, for the beginner, probably the best and most cost effective are those made by the French company, Opinel, whose well-known knife has a sturdy hardwood handle coupled to a carbon steel blade which takes and keeps a very good edge. More importantly when it comes to encouraging children to use knives, the blade has a locking facility to ensure you finish with the same number of fingers as when you started!

Sharpness is important; it is taught by many that a blunt blade will cause you more cuts than a sharp one because you have to apply more pressure… and then, when the blade slips, there's likely to be injuries. The blade should cut cleanly without undue pressure, once it does not it is time to sharpen. Purchase a fine carborundum type stone or, to get a really superb finish, an oil stone. The technique will take some practice, but very soon you can bring a dull blade back in a few seconds – little and often is the secret.

For whittling, in the manner of Mark Twain's 'loafers', there's nothing to stop you using any odd piece of available wood but, should you be thinking of producing a specific object or knick-knack, the type to be selected might be important. The choice is almost endless, from pieces saved from hedgerows to scraps of salvage from timber yards. You will soon develop an 'eye' for an interesting shape.

In general, the harder woods will give best results: they will undoubtedly be more difficult to work but will eventually have a smoother, more pleasing finish. Of the tropical hardwoods, most are superb, if you can get them. Rough pine, although readily available, is not terribly promising. From the hedgerow, blackthorn, hawthorn, ash, oak and lime are excellent. Whatever the type, check first that it does not contain any bad knots; they make cutting difficult.

Only your imagination limits what you can do. Practice, as in all things, makes perfect. Begin with something simple – and if you are intending going coarse fishing as a result of hearing about it elsewhere in this book, a fishing 'plug' is a good project. A plug is basically, made in the shape of a fish and fitted with a small eyelet at the front, to which the fishing line is fastened. Attached at the rear or on the underneath is a fishing hook. Gently drawn through the water, it acts as a lure to attract pike and other predatory fish.

Should fishing hold no interest, begin with a simple model of an animal such as a bear or otter, something of smooth lines which doesn't require too much detail. Don't worry about your failed attempts, you are learning and you will hardly have wasted a rain forest.

Whatever the subject chosen, it's a rule that in all carving that it's not about what you cut off, but what you leave behind that matters; patience and a good eye will help. Soon you may progress to walking stick handles and other useful items, but whatever you whittle, it will be unique and all your own work.

STICK-MAKING AND DRESSING

Every child loves to have a stick in their hand! It might be an imaginary sword, a crucial implement for poking about in a stream, a tool with which to knock the heads off thistles, or simply to rattle along a set of iron railings or a wooden fence where it creates a most satisfactory noise.

As a youngster grows, a stick is a useful walking aid for some serious outdoor exploration and, if curved at the end, might prove to be the perfect tool for pulling down high overhanging branches and collecting those out of reach blackberries and other hedgerow harvest. Harness this natural love of sticks and go out stick cutting – and then, once the sticks have 'seasoned', make a proper stick combining imagination and the element of danger caused by used 'adult' tools and penknives.

Cutting sticks is generally an autumn or winter activity, mainly because of the need to take them when the sap is at its lowest. Hazel is most stick-makers' wood of choice (particularly when using it as the shank for a shepherd's crook with a horn handle), but other useful sticks can be cut from ash and holly, and from both of these the bark should be peeled when cut. Blackthorn is another good one, though care must be taken when removing the sharp thorns that grow along its length.

Look out for straight branches growing from a cross-piece or at an angle from the trunk as these can often be used to create a natural handle. Some types of tree and shrubs (notably ash) have interesting roots which, dug carefully, can also make a great handle. For this reason, a small spade might be useful on your stick collecting expedition and, as well as a penknife, so too might be a good 'Bushman' saw and a cross-cut hand saw.

A stick should of course, be as straight as possible but its length is a matter of personal preference – and the eventual use for which it is intended. Having cut your stick, some patience is required as they then need to be taken home and dried for several months. Hang them head uppermost by string from a nail or rafter in the garage or shed: this allows the air to circulate. Once dry, depending on the type of wood being used, the shank needs preparation. For hazel and similar, it need only be smoothed down with fine sandpaper and then, when smooth, varnished over.

For shepherd's crook type sticks or thumb-sticks, a handle of ram's-horn is usually made for the former – and deer's-horn for the latter. Deer horn in particular is surprisingly easy to source out on a country walk as several deer species shed their antlers annually and so can be found just lying on the floor waiting for an enthusiastic stick maker. Affixing them to a shank is, however, somewhat more difficult but there are websites that give step-by-step instructions.

USING A POLE LATHE AND WORKING THINGS FROM GREENWOOD

Rural dads' of granddads' would almost certainly have known all about pole-lathes. As a means of turning wood, pole-lathes have certainly been around long before Viking times and were a practical tool much used in the countryside and elsewhere until the early 1950s. There has, though, been something of a recent revival in creating items of interest and practicality and there are nowadays regular courses for learning the art of pole-lathe turning and associated skills.

Wikipedia, that font of all knowledge on the most diverse of subjects, explains quite clearly and succinctly how a pole-lathe works:

'A pole lathe… uses a long pole as a return spring for a treadle. Pressing the treadle with your foot pulls on a cord that is wrapped around the piece of wood or billet being turned. The other end of the cord reaches up to the end of a long springy pole. As the action is reciprocating, the work rotates in one direction and then back the other way. Cutting is only carried out on the down stroke of the treadle, the spring of the pole only being sufficient to return the treadle to the raised position ready for the next down stroke. Modern pole lathes often replace the springy pole with an elastic bungee cord. While the action of the pole lathe and the skills required are similar to those employed on a modern power lathe, a requirement is that the timber used on a pole lathe is freshly felled and unseasoned, i.e., green.'

To help with the thought process regarding what possibly be made on a pole lathe, I include a few basic ideas here: rounders' bats; tool handles; garden dibbers; honey spoons; kitchen mixing bowls; stools and even models of insects and animals! Some farmyard animals are of a shape that lends themselves to being turned on a pole-lathe, pigs and sheep being possibly the most obvious. Drill holes in strategic places and then insert legs and antenna of dowel or twigs before painting and varnishing.

Even without a pole-lathe, it is possible for 'Team Granddad' to make some useful things from greenwood collected during an outdoors rural excursion. For example, a witch's broomstick is nothing but a shaft of cut and dried hazel with the bark removed and a 'head' of soft silver birch branches tightly bound to the shank by string or twisted wire. Practical as far as sweeping up the shed or removing the leaves from the lawn, no child can resist riding one hobby-horse style.

Greenwood can also make the frame for a saw-horse, to cut your winter wood to size and, if you were to make a simple saddle from an old cushion and add rope at one end for reins, it's the perfect mount for a budding jockey, show jumper or cowboy!

<u>**CHAPTER 12: SHARING IS CARING**</u>

Children love looking at old photos – to them, they might be ancient but to you, as a grandparent, they are memories of not all that long ago! Pictured wearing flared trousers, wide collared shirts and sporting long hair, such portraits of granddad will undoubtedly result in hoots of laughter and an incredulous 'is that really you?!'

Despite the risk of ridicule, photos on film rather than digital and scrapbooks kept for decades provide interesting social history. What treasures these personal files might hold – stamps; postcards; photographs – and maybe even the odd early teen 'love-letter' tucked safely away! Random in their compilation and held together with stamp hinges; photographic corners and yellowing sticky tape, their contents depict possibly important years of a person's life.

Perhaps several house moves notwithstanding, these reminders of times gone by always seem to remain long after other childhood items have been discarded. They may nowadays be stacked in boxes in the loft but they are there, ready to be rediscovered and, in the future, will undoubtedly show future generations what others got up to in their childhood.

The world is, however, constantly changing and, whereas a notebook would always have been the medium of choice (or, indeed, the only option), it's nowadays possible to record virtually anything on computers, iPhones and any amount of modern technology. But, no matter what the medium, why not continue with the scrapbook tradition?

Jeanne Wines-Reed and Joan Wines in their book, *Scrapbooking for Dummies* suggest that, before you start, you should spend some time in preparation and decide upon its intended purpose. Fully understanding both your general and specific aims and objectives helps enormously in deciding what is extraneous – and what is essential. These could include current projects; intended ones for the future – or simply observations based on what today's granddads used to do in their own childhood. There's room for some 'out-of-the-box' thinking too... what did you learn from your grandfather – and what rapidly disappearing skills would you like to pass on to your grandchildren's generation.

To help achieve that, grandparents willing to spend time doing so, might well consider 'going back to school' for the benefit of their grandchildren and their classmates.

Shy granddads who may be nervous about standing up in front of a classroom of children and talking at length about a particular topic could instead be interviewed by the class – and the information gained subsequently written up as a school newspaper article or as a cross curricular piece of writing comparing cultural and technological changes between then and now.

A list of typical questions might well include:

* When were you born, and where?

* Where did you live while you were growing up?

* What was your favourite toy as a child? What were some other popular toys of the time?

* Did you have to do any chores? What were they?

* What types of things did you and your family do for entertainment?

* How did you get to school each morning?

* What do you remember about your teachers, your classroom, or the subjects you learned?

* What types of games did you play outside at break-times?

* How does our school compare to the one you went to as a boy?

* Were there any major events in history which occurred while you were young and may have affected our lives today?

Alternatively, the information can be collected from interviews and written up and illustrated for a class book about their granddads. These should include what, in the child's eyes, make their particular granddad special, what activities they like to do with their granddads, a favourite memory of them – and how they think they will be when they are themselves a grandparent many years hence!

Before such visits can take place, there might, though, be a need to think about any possible child care safety issues demanded by the state. In Britain, for instance, there is the legal requirement for any persons (including volunteers) to have been checked by the Disclosure and Barring Service (DBS) – which was, until June 2015, previously known as a 'CRB' (The Criminal Records Bureau) check. UK schools are not, however, required to apply for a DBS check if the volunteer is supervised at all times and does not come into school regularly (i.e.; more than once a week) so there's likely to be very little preventing granddad from going back to school after an absence of several decades!

How lucky the grandchild with an attentive and fun-orientated granddad. Conversely, how lucky the grandparent with a grandchild ready and willing to appreciate the love, care and subtle education they unconditionally offer.

To be a 'dangerous' granddad it's not necessary to be always adventurous – as one sprightly septuagenarian who stills spends much of his time cycling and mountain hiking recently pointed out: 'You don't need to take them up Ben Nevis to teach them survival skills. Even if you're not an outdoors enthusiast, taking your grandchildren camping in the back garden will give them cherished memories.'

Unexpected fun is always important – the most surprising the better! Not long before he died in 2017, David Shepherd, wildlife artist, conservationist, grandfather and great-grandfather, remembered that: '80 years ago, when I was a little boy Granddad was Archdeacon of Bodmin and his work took up much of his time as his life was devoted to his profession. However, I have a strong memory of one particular moment when the front door burst open and in walked my grandfather (in all his full clerical regalia) calling out; "Let's go to the fair and ride on the dodgems!"'

And, on that note, I think we can all say 'Amen'!